THE PEOPLE FACTOR
Giving People Top Priority in the
Life and Ministry of the Local Church

by
Oral Withrow

Warner Press Ministries
Anderson, Indiana

Scripture quotations, unless otherwise indicated, are from the Holy Bible, New Revised Standard Version, 1989, Grand Rapids: Zondervan Bible Publishers.

© 1996 by Warner Press
ISBN #0-87162-792-2 Stock # D5201
UPC #730817 203355

All rights reserved
Printed in the United States of America
Warner Press, Inc

David C. Shultz, Editor in Chief
Arthur Kelly, BRIDGES Editor
Dan Harman, Project Editor
Cover by Curtis D. Corzine

Contents

Foreword   x

Introduction   xii

Chapter 1: People Are Priority   1

People are much alike and much different. All are on a pilgrimage but they are at different places in their pilgrimages—spiritual as well as personal, vocational, and family. It is integral to the ministry of the local church that it recognize the variety of its people and help them find direction.

Chapter 2: Ways to Keep People First   16

Five words help the church keep a focus on people: know people, relate to people, serve people, love people, reconcile people. Suggestions are made on how to take each action.

Chapter 3: The Sin/Grace Factor   33

The good news is that the Bible defines sin and tells us that forgiveness is wonderful, grace is a marvelous continuing experience, and God provides power for victory over sin.

Chapter 4: The Illness/Healing Factor   48

People participating in the life of the local congregation are in need of healing. It is not some people, or a few people, or an occasional person. People are hurting in a variety of ways but they are all hurting sometime in some way. It is, therefore, absolutely necessary that a church discover ways to minister to suffering people through prayer, biblically based counseling, and correct teaching on the whole subject of divine healing.

Chapter 5: The Vocation Factor   71

Is God's will individual, personal, and unique? Is God's call to any and all who will respond and in ways they may choose? The answer is yes! The call of God on our lives is both specific and general. It is with the dual experience of divine call that many of us need help. God has a general will for the church, also, and a specific call to ministry for each congregation.

Chapter 6: The Time Factor   83

Each person has a limited number of hours to give to the local church for any purpose. The number of responsibilities one person can handle is limited. The organizational structure of the local church can dictate a misuse of the time members can give in ministry. Suggestions are made on how to focus on ministry even in board and committee meetings.

Chapter 7: The Pastor Person   99

The greatest mistake pastors make about themselves is this one: they forget they are human. The biggest mistake that churches make about their pastors is this one: they forget their pastors are human. Several perspectives—vocational, personal, spiritual—are given on this critical church problem with observations on the superhuman pastoral assignment.

Chapter 8: When the Fur Flies   119

Conflict is inevitable in any group of people, including the church. This chapter considers the basic kinds of conflict found in churches and suggests ways of dealing with them. It raises important questions about unity and looks carefully at what the Bible teaches about confession and forgiveness.

Contents

Chapter 9: The Freedom Factor 136

People need freedom. Freedom is not a license to do as we please. It is liberty to live and function within broad parameters. Legalism sets boundaries about everything and prescribes how life shall be lived. Freedom is not only permission to think and act within certain broad boundaries; freedom is also the created climate for personal discovery, decision making, and growth. Freedom for forgiveness and freedom for a variety of spiritual exercises is essential.

Chapter 10: More Freedom 153

Six more freedoms characteristic of biblically based fellowship and a caring community of believers: freedom to know and accept each other; freedom for ministry; freedom to decide without coercion; freedom within the fellowship; freedom of conscience; and freedom to be a pilgrim.

Chapter 11: Sinners, Sliders, Saints, and the Slighted 178

Builders, Boomers, and Busters are sociological age groups to which the church will find ways to minister. Another way the church may look at people is as Sinners: Group #1: ones who have not accepted Christ as savior; Sinners #2: persons who have been committed to Christ but who have broken that relationship; Saints #1: exemplary Christians; Saints #2: faithful followers of Christ whose example and humble spirit are known less broadly; the Slighted: those who are slighted by society and, tragically, slighted by the church.

Bibliography 199

FOREWORD

Some have jokingly remarked, "The church would be great if it just weren't for all the people." Not so, for the church is people. Oral Withrow has caught the essence of what effective ministry is all about in his new book, *The People Factor*. If you are interested in effective transformational ministry, you will want to study and share this book with the people in your church. Pastors and congregations that are making a difference have learned that people, not programs, doctrine, finances, or administration, must come first.

I have devoted my life to being a student of effective pastors and congregations. In my twenty-five years of pastoring, I have had the unique privilege of being associated with some of the most effective churches and pastors in America today. Some of the churches are megachurches and some are much smaller, but they all have one key ingredient in common: they give people a top priority in the life and ministry of the local church.

Oral Withrow challenges some of the traditions and myths that have often hindered effective ministry. He relates practical insights out of his own rich experience of pastoring and ministering to pastors and congregations across America. His Ponder and Process section at the end of each chapter makes this book a practical tool to use with small groups and classes for congregations who are wanting to make their ministry more effective.

Foreword

I have found in my own experience that all ministry in the church flows out of relationships. If I could summarize the essence of Christ's teaching in just one word, it would be relationship. He came to bring us into right relationship with God and right relationship with each other. That is what the good news is really all about. *The People Factor* relates some very practical principles on how to build and maintain those relationships in the life of the church. This is one book that really needed to be written.

Ray Cotton
Senior Pastor
New Hope Community Church
Portland, Oregon

Introduction

> *Jesus went throughout Galilee, teaching in their synagogues and proclaiming the good news of the kingdom and curing every disease and every sickness among the people.*
> —Matthew 4:23

Jesus moved among the people, telling them of God's love and salvation and ministering to them. Later he would commission the twelve disciples to do the same (Matthew 10). The New Testament is a guide for the church, the body of Christ, to sustain ministry to people.

The church has developed many statements of doctrine, established hundreds of traditions, created thousands of organizations, erected innumerable buildings, and sanctioned a wide variety of personal interpretations of the faith. Most of these statements, traditions, and organizations have been essential, helpful, and a blessing. Even a casual reading of Christian history, however, will show that some have been negative in intent and results. Whether beneficial or detrimental, creeds, traditions, and organizations are not the purpose of the church. To be sure, they have often become the focus of denominations, movements, and congregations.

In each generation, congregations are challenged to respond to the living Christ in their midst and rediscover their essential ministry—to people. The second generation of Christians in the seven churches of Asia was faced with dire alternatives if they did not rediscover their original purpose (Revelation 2–3).

This book affirms the essentials of the Faith—salvation by faith through grace, discipleship, sound doctrine, and servant ministry—but observes that the energies of the church are often dissipated on functions of the organization; the needs of people, both the members and the unconverted, become secondary. Suggestions are offered on ways for keeping people first in the life and ministry of the church, encouraging persons to accept grace, providing for healing, responding individually and corporately to God's call by using time, caring for pastors, handling conflict, structuring for freedom, and taking care of the slighted. The intent is to focus on people—the people factor is most important in the ministry of the church.

In the **Ponder and Process** section at the end of each chapter the reader is asked to take *action* and is provided with questions and thoughts for *meditation*. A guide for group consideration is identified as a *"Discussion Process"* and is a suitable outline for small groups, conferences, and Sunday school classes.

Chapter 1

PEOPLE ARE PRIORITY

Clay Avenue is one block long. Our home was in the middle at 1632 and Mr. Bailey's neighborhood grocery store was at one end, right next to the steep gravel road that led down to the bus stop. We had begun buying groceries often at the new supermarkets, Kroger's and A & P, on opposite corners of West Washington Street at Stockton Avenue. Day-to-day purchases were still made at Mr. Bailey's store—bread, lunch meat, and milk—and we still placed purchases "on the book." Dad now had a regular job as a laborer at the brickyard but the Depression had depleted family finances and there were six of us children, including my three older brothers who were in high school.

The grocery store was small with a soft drink cooler on the right when you entered and on wall shelves were canned goods and packages that Mr. Bailey retrieved item by item when you indicated what you wanted. The place that he waited on you was toward the back and that is where our book was among the books of many others who charged items. All of that for me was incidental. What was important to me was the walnut and glass display case that was to the left as you entered the store: it was the candy case.

When Dad's payday came, either Mom or my big sister Juanita would take some money to Mr. Bailey to pay on the bill. When the bill was "paid down some," Mr. Bailey would say, "Let's go around to the candy counter and get ten cents worth of candy. You can pick it out." Then it was my turn to choose most of the candy, though my baby sister Carma Lee would indicate her favorite pieces. The candy case was a marvel to me with Tootsie Rolls, coconut ribbons, jaw-breakers, B-B Bats (chocolate, banana, and strawberry), chocolate creams, and small Baby Ruths, Butterfingers, Mr. Goodbars, to mention a few. Carma Lee and I, with our noses barely over the bottom level of the candy counter, would point and Mr. Bailey would fill up the little bag with our choices.

It was then that a fantasy began to form in my mind that would expand over the years. As I matured and became an adult, my candy fantasy was repressed, but it was always there.

A half century later I was the guest of the Mount Scott Church in Portland, Oregon, and entertained myself one Saturday afternoon by walking through the Clackamas Mall. I strolled in and out of stores and then found myself in the middle of my fantasy that had been developing for decades. Before me were transparent containers of candy from the floor to the ceiling, on every wall and in the center of the store. Chocolates, fruit-flavored hard candy, soft chewy candy, candy in every color of the rainbow, candy in every size imaginable. My childhood fantasy was realized, and I smiled.

The candy store experience was sensuous—my eyes saw, my nose smelled, and my hands touched. I strolled around the store for almost an hour; finally, with a bit of discipline, I purchased a small quantity of two candies. I hoped I hadn't been a bother to the hired help but the variety of candies on display captivated my consciousness.

Like the diversity of candies in my fantasy, the diversity of people in the local church is awesome. Some persons you are immediately attracted too; others you have to "acquire a taste for." You could say that people are different in some of the same ways that candies are different: some are tart, some sweet, some strong, and some mild. It is a marvelous experience to see people, speak with people, touch people, and realize the infinite variety of personalities and qualities present in a group.

I am becoming more and more aware that people are the primary factor in the life of the church. People are so much alike, all children of God, and so different, unique in many ways. In most congregations you will find

• people with a short fuse and others who are unignitable;

• people who always nod their heads up and down and others who habitually shake their head left to right to left;

• people who smile all the time and several who rarely smile;

• people who are present for every event and those who show up occasionally;

- people who consider everything in logical order and others who never seem to be on the same subject as the rest of the group;
- people who think before speaking and several who do not know what they think until they hear themselves say it;
- people for whom problems are a source of challenge and energy and persons who are totally disturbed and disrupted by problems in the fellowship;
- people who bring dysfunctional behaviors of their families into the church family and others who have healthy family backgrounds;
- people who are paranoid, who think nobody likes them and everyone is talking about them; others who believe everyone loves them and cannot conceive that anyone may not love them;
- people who are a delight to be around and people who are a pain-in-the-neck;
- people who do well in everything they attempt and people who do one or two things well but have had many obvious failures;
- people who appear, at least, to understand and live with a spiritual orientation and others who never seem aware of more than their own physical and material needs.

All of these people are on a pilgrimage; in addition, they are at different places in their pilgrimages—spiritual as well as personal, vocational, and family. They have accepted Christ as Savior and Lord and have given themselves to the community of believers.

Many other wonderful persons in each church who are not believers are weighing the possibility of taking that step.

It is integral to the ministry of the local church that it recognize the variety of personalities, family histories, and life experiences of its people. Understanding people and helping them find direction and solve problems is a key to effective ministry and enjoyable fellowship in the life of a congregation.

> **People Are Different**
> **Extroverts** relate more to the outer world of things, people, and environment.
> They ask the question, "How do I relate to what is going on out there?" Their primary source of interest and energy comes from the outer world. Extroverts feel a loss of energy if they engage in too much introspection.
> **Introverts** prefer to relate more to the inner world of idea, concepts, and feelings.
> They ask the question, "How does what is going on out there relate to me?" Energy expended relating to the outer world returns when introverts are alone and can look inside themselves.
> —Oswald and Kroeger (2–3)

The Gospel Says Who

The gospel is not overly concerned with *what* or *how*.

Even *when* is seldom specific but is more concerned with a general time. "Now is the day of salvation!" (2 Corinthians 6:2) does not refer so much to, say, Thursday, October 12, as it does to a broader time of the Lord's provision.

Where is not of little importance in the gospel because the scriptures insist that God is at work everywhere and the message of forgiveness and hope is for every nation.

The gospel focuses on *Who!* The address is made to whoever believes (John 3:15–16; Acts 10:43); the requirements for discipleship are the same for any follower (Matthew 16:24). People are the focus of the New Testament Gospels. The Acts of the Apostles and the letters written by the apostles retain the same orientation to people. The Bible identifies who spoke the message of the resurrection of Jesus Christ, who responded to that message, and how all those persons got together to live out that message. The scriptures identify cultural characteristics of those who believed—Jews, Greeks, men, women, and sometimes their citizenship—from Tarsus, or Rome, or Jerusalem.

Who is the focus of the gospel and it continues to be the focus of the church. Unfortunately, people may be forgotten in a preoccupation with other factors of church life. We will identify some of those factors after we look at how Jesus brought tradition and people into proper perspective.

Matthew 12:1–8

Why is it necessary to affirm that people are priority in the church? Because the church, like nations, families and communities, forgets that people are more important than rules, regulations, traditions, and laws. The religious leaders in Jesus' day forgot it. They rebuked Jesus for allowing his followers to pluck wheat to eat. Why was it wrong for them to eat? They were eating on the Sabbath, a day for worship. It was a good religious law, a day reserved for worship. But it was not the primary law.

The people were hungry and Jesus pointed out to the religious leaders that the Sabbath was made for people, not people for the Sabbath. His statement upset them. They knew people were the priority. The scriptures that they memorized with reverence taught that God created people as the culmination of all God's creative work and did it because God wanted to relate to something, somebody. Somewhere along the way, priorities had gotten mixed up and the Sabbath became more important than people. Myron Augsburger says, "Jesus showed us that human need takes precedence over rites, codes or cultural taboos" (Augsburger 152).

The theme of Matthew 12 is the lordship of Christ. One of the controversies that is used to demonstrate this is the Sabbath controversy. When Jesus is challenged for letting his disciples work on the Sabbath by harvesting grain, even if it be for a snack, Jesus responds in the style of argument or debate with which they are familiar.

First, he recalls the story of David and his followers eating the bread of the Presence, strictly prohibited by law. Jesus and his accusers are aware this is not the strongest part of his argument. David is a special person and he and his men were desperate for food. Jesus' disciples, however, were probably only on a Sabbath's day walk and, though Matthew indicates they were hungry, their hunger was not critical. Their hunger is not the point anyway.

Second, he points out the obvious: No one is permitted to work on the Sabbath, but the priests in the performance of their duties do work on the Sabbath. It was generally understood that the priestly function superseded the Sabbath law. Thus Jesus, in his debate wins a point, for it is agreed that there are times and situations when principles are higher than the law.

> **People and Disciplines**
> In the evangelicalism with which I am familiar the emphasis on discipline has at times gotten out of hand. Such emphasis is sometimes placed on the disciplines of devotion, Bible study, prayer, fellowship, and witnessing or personal evangelism, that these good obediences begin to obscure simpler ones such as honest conversation with another person ... openness to the opinion of others, time for perhaps unstrategic persons (such as parents and family) ... concern for social justice.... People are eclipsed by disciplines in some forms of disciplined Christianity.
> —Frederick Bruner (448)

Third, Jesus then insists that a whole new principle of evaluation is being introduced. His words assert his own lordship of the Sabbath. Some scholars suggest that the assertion is more subtle in the original language—the words used by Jesus affirm a principle more than his person. Either way, the Sabbath laws are relegated to a lesser value than the needs of people (Augsburger, Carson, Barclay). As Frederick Bruner has commented:

> The point of the law is not the scrupulous self-sacrifice you derive from it; it is the wide-hearted humanity the

prophets make of it. 'I desire mercy and not sacrifice' means I desire heart not will, human sympathy not super-human disciplines, personalism not perfectionism.

(Bruner 448)

The Pharisees understood what he was saying; his argument was well put. They only had to read their own tradition (M. Hagigah 1:8): "The rules about the Sabbath ... are as mountains hanging by a hair, for Scripture is scanty and the rules many" (Carson 279). The story, the accusations of the Pharisees, and Jesus' response to these sincere persons also suggest to us that many of our traditions may be based more on rules than on scripture.

People of the world are priority. We have been tempted at times to think our nation is the most important entity in the world. At other times some have presumed that Caucasians are more important than people of color. Many are convinced that people with wealth, particularly property, have greater value than poor people. Most groups are convinced that "we" are more important than "they." An excellent standard of living for some is often deemed more important than the need for food, shelter, and medicine for others. "They will soon be taking everything we have" is the fearful warning. Christians are tempted to voice the ideal, yet in practical matters, such as politics, act in the interests of the few—taxes, welfare, entitlements are scorned and privileges granted to the wealthy. The world often has to be reminded that all people are priority—their needs are a major and not an incidental concern.

> **What Are Human Beings?**
> O LORD, our Sovereign,
>   how majestic is your name in all the earth!
> You have set your glory above the heavens.
> Out of the mouths of babes and infants
>   you have founded a bulwark because of your foes,
>   to silence the enemy and the avenger.
> When I look at your heavens, the work of your fingers,
>   the moon and the stars that you have established;
>   what are human beings that you are mindful of them,
>   mortals that you care for them?
> Yet you have made them a little lower than God,
>   and crowned them with glory and honor.
>
> You have given them dominion over the works of your hands;
>   you have put all things under their feet,
>   all sheep and oxen,
>   and also the beasts of the field,
>   the birds of the air, and the fish of the sea,
>   whatever passes along the paths of the seas.
> O LORD, our Sovereign,
>   how majestic is your name in all the earth.
> —Psalm 8

People are the priority in the family. Husbands are important, wives are important, and children are important. It is so easy to postpone that understanding, disregard it, forget it. Jobs become priority, eclipsing spouses and children. Abstract and ill-informed concepts of self-fulfillment can lead to a neglect of relationships. A preoccupation with money leads to a valuing of people according to earning power.

Performance can be the basis of receiving approval or unbearable disapproval, and valuing a person for being themselves is lost. All people have a critical need to be in a familial group where they are appreciated for who they are and not what they can do.

The Other Factors

Three of us high school boys were invited, for some purpose I cannot recall, into the living room of a couple in our community. It was communicated in some way that we were to talk quietly while there, or at least we had that impression. A dish of sweets was passed in front of us with the instruction to take one. The most amazing thing to us was that all the furniture was covered; the couch where we sat had a sheet over it and various other pieces had coverings. Somehow we knew, from our mothers or others, that the furniture stayed covered all the time. The conversation had to do with what the couple wanted us to do. I do not recall that they asked us anything about ourselves or indicated any interest in our concerns. When the conversation ended and the reason for our being there was completed, we suggested that we had better leave. We had a good laugh as we hurried down the sidewalk. Of this we were convinced: the couple were very interested in keeping their lives and home undisturbed. They were very protective of their furniture, stingy with their cookies, did not trust us very much, and wanted to use us in some way. We were equally convinced that we did not want to be involved with them more than to wave at them occasionally from across the street. We knew that we were not of great importance to them, or, if we were, they did not know how to tell us.

Local churches have at times been accused of being just as protective of furniture and buildings. They sometimes express concern in measured doses, and, yes, they sometimes insist that people be quiet. Some churches are guilty of using persons more than relating to them. The church is tempted to forget to focus on people.

People are priority in the church. The church has often forgotten people. Following are some of the things that often take precedence over people:

> The *truth*, that is, *doctrine*, often takes precedence. The body of belief becomes something that is more precious to preachers, theologians, and others long-in-the-faith. Doctrine is written to help people understand the teachings of the Word.
> Doctrine is a guide for a spiritual journey. It is not an instrument by which to exclude or to punish people. The truth of the gospel and doctrinal teachings are of great value but legalism elevates both over people. The gospel focuses on the needs of people and doctrine is a tool of discipleship, for the purpose of informing and instructing people of the church.
> *Tradition* also at times takes precedence over people in the church. This does not occur in every church; some diligently hold the values of tradition but as a servant to people, not the dominating factor. The way ministry has been done to meet human needs in the past can be sustained, and thus we fail to adapt our ministries to meet the needs of persons we now have an opportunity to serve in the community.

Programs can be traditions rather than ministries. Often originally organized to meet the real needs of people, some programs no longer serve people. Such programs are often untouchable—sacred cows that cannot be changed.

Organizational structures, committees, membership or leadership groups, and even the names of programs can become functionally more important than people.

Buildings, of all things, can become more important than people. The preservation of facilities can be the principal concern of the annual budget. When members think of church they often are picturing facilities, architectural constructs that are beautiful to the eye. Who of us, to be sure, does not respond and appreciate art and form. Buildings, however, may be closed so that walls, and halls, paint and chairs are not stained, abused, or damaged. Gyms may be reserved for members and food preparation facilities for church affairs. (You will read later about a congregation that put their gymnasium to use by people.) Church leaders will want to consider the wisdom in words attributed to Winston Churchill: "We shape our buildings; thereafter they shape us."

Ego needs of a leader can become more important than people. People thus are tools for the leader. The leader may be a pastor who needs persons to applaud her or his performance or be an extension of the pastor's personality. Just as often the leader may be a layperson who must control people or make them so uncomfortable that they leave.

I wish I could say these factors are not a part of the church and that they are only a part of the world and some dysfunctional families. But these factors are very much a part of some congregations. My concern is that doctrine, tradition, buildings, and the ego needs of leaders are often more at the heart of a local congregation than people. Though these are important, people are the most important factor in the church. It was for people that Christ died—sinners even.

> **Romans 5:8–9**
> But God proves his love for us in that while we still were sinners Christ died for us. Much more surely then, now that we have been justified by his blood, will we be saved through him from the wrath of God.

Therefore:
- The church exists as a community (a group of people) for worship.
- It intentionally tells people of the love of God in Christ.
- The church helps believers (people) grow in their understanding of the faith.
- The church guides persons in the discovery of their unique talents and spiritual gifts and prepares them to serve other people.
- The church seeks out people who have physical, emotional, and spiritual needs and serves them in the name of Jesus.
- The church celebrates the diversity and unity of the body (people) of Christ.

People are the priority in the church!

On the following pages we will indicate practical ways to put people first in the life and ministry of the local church.

Ponder and Process

Action Process

Ask three friends, "What or who do you think is given the highest priority in our church: tradition, the building, or people?"

Ask family members, "What is our family's highest priority?"

Meditation Process

Do people understand you? Appreciate you? Why or why not?

Discussion Process

Read Matthew 12:1–8 or tell the story. Review the interpretation provided in chapter 1.

Enlist three persons who are not easily threatened to lead a group discussion about the personality differences of the three. Ask the three to respond individually to the group's evaluation, explaining how they felt or what they had already known or didn't know about themselves. Ask others to indicate how their individuality affects participation in the life of the church.

Or pose to the group this question: How does a congregation give appropriate emphasis to doctrine, tradition, buildings, and to pastoral and lay leadership and yet remain primarily focused on ministry to people?

Conclude by reading Psalm 8; before the session begins ask a member of the group to prepare to read this psalm. Pray the Lord's prayer in unison.

Chapter 2

STRATEGIES TO KEEP PEOPLE FIRST

Five words can help us keep people first in the mind and ministry of the local church:

> *Know* people
> *Relate* to people
> *Serve* people
> *Love* people
> *Reconcile* people

1. Know People

People are a priority to us, as individuals and as a church, when we take time to know them. Again, this seems so rudimentary that it is not necessary to state it. Yet is not uncommon for us to speak of and relate to people as if they are disembodied souls or persons without a past or personalities whose only dimension is the spiritual or ideal. Students of psychology have developed several models that help us understand the various needs of persons. Though humanistic in basic approach, Abraham Maslow provided a model for understanding the needs of people, my needs as well as those of others. He stacked them in a pyramid but emphasized that no single need is more important than another. Physiological needs (survival and safety) must be met before energy can be directed toward, for instance, personal esteem.

Here is the way Maslow constructed the model:

(Maslow, in *Craig*, 48)

It is not our intent to identify the best psychological models, rather, only to give a sample. The model demonstrates that we are all complex personalities. For any of us to serve another in a significant way, we must recognize our common needs. We risk injuring persons when we fail to recognize each has many needs.

We may want to utilize more of the insights of psychologists and pollsters later, but now it is sufficient for us to use pop psychology phrases to indicate what we need to know for sure about all of us.

a. You and I have *basic physical and social needs.* If either of us fails to recognize and honor the need for food, shelter, clothing, and medicine, then we fail to recognize each other's humanness. Persons have human needs that cannot be ignored.

Seven Needs

Every pastor should know at least seven needs of the average American:

1. The need for shelter and food.
2. The need to believe life is meaningful and has a purpose (70 percent of respondents).
3. The need for a sense of community and deeper relationships.
4. The need to be appreciated and respected.
5. The need to be listened to and be heard.
6. The need to feel one is growing in faith.
7. The need for practical help in developing a mature faith.

—George Gallup, Jr (1)

---

b. You and I want to be *valued.* When I was a teenager I read in a newspaper the observation, "Every one has a sign on his or her chest that says, 'I WANT TO FEEL IMPORTANT!' " That does not mean that we are all self-centered. It is a part of being human to want to know we are valued. The wise church finds ways of communicating to every person who participates in its fellowship that "You are important!" You will notice that Jesus made the adulteress, the tax collector, and the persons who felt unworthy of healing realize that they were indeed important to him and God.

c. You and I want to find *meaning in life.* The psychologist often calls this self-actualization. Meaning or self-actualization denotes the person is, from the Christian point of view, realizing the purpose for which God created him or her; from the psychological point of view, approaching full development of one's potential. Either way, it is a tremendous satisfaction for anyone to realize in some measure, "I do count for something," and "My life has made a difference."

> **Most Visitors in Crisis**
> Most visitors or inactive members who show up in your congregation (except on high holy days!) have been going through some crisis.... Visiting in their homes reading notes from the deacons' welcome phone calls, even greeting at the door—I would become aware of a recent move, a career change, a parent in a nursing home, an infertile couple, a stillborn child, a lover's or a parent's crisis.... The world breaks everyone.... Even a handshake at the door would become a prayer.
> We should be training our pastors and lay visitors and phone callers and people in the pews to listen ... for tips of these submerged crises. It would change our prayers—our programs.
> —Kent Ira Groff (7)

One simple discipline that is essential to communicating a person's value: know the person's name. When that discipline is practiced in the church and the community, persons feel we know them. When we do not know people's names we send a message that people do not matter. Many viewers of the television series M.A.S.H. will recall that the character Radar often insisted on being called Walter. His name meant something. His nickname indicated his ability to hear helicopters coming before anyone else did. Walter wanted to be appreciated for more than his auditory gift. When nicknames (such as Shorty, Baldy, and Fats) are derogatory, they communicate a lack of knowledge of the person. Such a simple thing as calling a person by the correct name and refusing to make light of his or her identity communicates that we really know that person.

2. Relate to People

We indicate a high priority on people in the church when we relate to them. Children and adults identify with the story of Jesus' encounter with Zacchaeus. The tax collector was not popular with most people since he represented a conqueror and local officials whom they felt were unjust. He was also short, and when Jesus came to Jericho Zacchaeus had to climb a tree to get a better view. Jesus stopped, walked under the tree, looked up and said, as the children's song words it, "Zacchaeus, you come down, for I'm going to your house for tea." That is relating.

To relate means to communicate. Talking is a part of communication. It is amazing to realize that so many of us in church say so little to one another. It takes effort and it takes time. For some reason many of us are afraid of sounding ridiculous. Refusal to say something communicates either that I do not want to relate or that I do not value relationships highly enough to take the risk of speaking. Asking about the weather, or "How are you doing?" or remarking, "I saw you yesterday at the shopping center" are simple and obvious statements, but they are valid ways of starting a conversation. Speaking to someone else in such a fashion communicates a desire to relate and a response recognizes that the person speaking has value; it is only a minor risk of starting a conversation. Too many people in too many churches do not take the simple initiative to talk. Therefore, aloofness and coldness are communicated even though the silent person may be compassionate and concerned. Relating does mean that we talk—communicate.

> **Cum Panis**
> I believe that we are placed here to be companions—a wonderful word that comes from **cum panis** ("with bread"). We are here to share bread with one another so that everyone has enough, no one has too much and our social order achieves this goal with maximal freedom and minimal coercion.
> —Robert McAfee Brown (5)

To communicate also means that we *listen*, an even more difficult skill. Listening can seldom be done in a hurry. I have friends who have never listened to a word I've said; that is the way I feel anyway. They say something to me and then when I begin to respond they look away or walk away. They have said what is on their minds and have communicated to me that they have little interest in what I think. (Since I am the father of four children, I know that I am not guiltless in this matter, or so I have been told.)

Relating in the church means that we consciously, individually, corporately, and with discipline learn to listen to new people and to members—both to pastors and laypersons. Business meetings sometimes become chaotic because persons have not listened. They have presumed what another was going to say and the presumption was so strong that every word spoken was heard in a different way than the speaker meant.

For instance one pastor suggested a congregation increase its giving to missions. A woman stood to object, for she knew the pastor meant "to direct more money to his pet projects." A layleader inquired in a building committee meeting about the necessity of building all the facilities at once. "Why can't we do it in phases?" he asked. The pastor responded, "Why can't we trust the Lord and take the risks of doing something significant; why do we always have to do things half way?" In both instances the people did not listen. Therefore, relationships were disrupted and in both instances good relationships were essential to the ministry tasks of the church.

Stephen Covey speaks of *empathic listening*. His instructions for highly effective people have much to say to Christians and congregations that want to relate more effectively. Covey explains that we usually listen at one of four levels. One level is ignoring what the other is saying. A second level of listening is pretending and responding with phrases such as, "Yeah, uh-huh. Right." The third level is selective listening, for instance, as to the chatter of a very young child. A higher level is attentive listening where we focus on the words that are spoken.

Covey challenges us to the highest form, empathic listening, which he defines as "listening to understand ... listening [that] gets inside another person's frame of reference ... you see the world the way they see the world, you understand their paradigm, you understand how they feel" (Covey, 240).

Community

The best-selling author Scott Peck explains that every where he travels in the United States he finds at once both a lack of community and a thirst for community. He emphasizes that it is particularly distrubing to discover a lack of community in churches. Peck defines community as "a group of individuals who have learned how to communicate honestly with each other, whose relationships go deeper than their masks of composure, and who have developed some significant commitment to 'rejoice together, mourn together,' and to 'delight in each other, make others' conditions our own.' "

—Scott Peck (57, 59)

Bonding is another way we relate in healthful ways to people in the church as in other groups. Bonding is principally the act of being-with. The first stories of the early Christians include this telling statement, "All who believed were together" (Acts 2:44a).

One New Testament writer insists that Christians err when they neglect getting together regularly—bonding (Hebrew 10:25). Forming small groups is one way that many churches have enabled bonding, recognizing that many persons, unless they have nearby close family, need opportunity to be together a sufficient time to permit relationships to develop.

3. Serve People

Jesus said to both his adversaries and his disciples, "The greatest among you will be your servant" (Matthew 23:11). In the fellowship of the church we serve people in at least two ways:

Help
When a thorn pierces the foot, the whole body must bend over to pull it out.
—Zulu proverb (*Context*, 5)

The first is with *help*. The Christian perspective is usually distinctly different from that common in our culture. It is a temptation in the church to use people to help us achieve our goals and relieve our pain or stress. It is reasonable to expect help from others in the fellowship but it is essential that each in the fellowship develop both the attitude and discipline of helping others. Long-distance help is through offerings for missions and in response to disasters. Long-distance helping and community service are not the only ministries of the local church. A readiness to respond to the hurts of members and worship attenders is essential. Bill and Gloria Gaither have not been idealistic in their description of "The Family of God." What they have said indicates a quality of the fellowship in the church: we do cry and rejoice with each other; whatever our life situation we are rich because we 'belong" to the family of God.

A second way we serve is with *hope*. Encouragement is an assignment given each of us. A compliment on clothing, an observation about a success reported in the paper, an assurance of prayer as another person faces surgery or a major decision, thanks for a song or a special effort for the group, recognition for service, notes of affection, and, as mentioned above, time taken just to talk, are all ways of encouraging others in the church.

Hope is integral to the worship, the learning situations, and the fellowship events of the church. The gospel gives us a new chance. Joyce Hoak, a veteran primary-grades teacher, brought hope to all ages during her presentation to children in a Sunday morning worship. The children sat at her feet in the chancel area as she took from a sack a children's toy that can be written or drawn upon. When one wants to clear the screen all of the marks disappear. Joyce explained that when we have made a mistake we can erase our errors and start over again. She noted, however, that on the screen she had erased there were still some smudges. She explained very simply that sometimes when we have treated someone wrongly, we still have this feeling deep inside that is not a good feeling. Joyce then produced a clean sheet of paper. She explained that God helps us wipe the slate clean when we have done wrong but, even better, when we feel wrong inside, God will give us a clean sheet of paper—inside ourselves we can be totally forgiven.

That is hope. It is hope for children in their sense of guilt for error. It is just as important for adults. It is the message of the gospel—God loves us and forgives us.

We serve well when we tell and remind each other that our sins can be forgiven. All of us need that hope.

4. Love People

Love is the most difficult assignment of all, for it requires that we look not only at our acts and words, but our attitudes. It often requires that the concerns of another be elevated above our own. Jesus said, "You shall love your neighbor as yourself" and only the love of God has precedence (Mark 12:31). Jesus presumes we love ourselves and that we will give attention to our personal needs.

Love is multidimensional and all that we have said before about knowing people and relating to people are aspects of the love relationship. Most of what is suggested in this book is a guide toward demonstrating love in the congregation of believers and then demonstrating love in the community—to all persons. Demonstrating love includes words of respect, actions that help persons who are suffering, and services that help people learn to meet their own needs. One dimension of love is essential and often difficult in the life of the church, or any group, and it is to that aspect of love that we give brief attention.

Love is *liking* someone. It is easy to separate loving and liking, particularly when we think of certain people. I often wonder how some people feel about me when they, usually in letters, say something about "loving me in Christian love" or signing correspondence, "Love in Christ." Often it is an effort to express affection without any sexual overtones. Too often it is a way, in the life of the congregation, of meeting the requirement of Christ that we love a person while at the same time freeing ourselves to sustain attitudes of distaste for the person. Perhaps we should acknowledge that some persons aggravate us by their lifestyle or attitude. But Jesus would encourage us to like each other, especially other persons in the church.

> **Emotional Complaints**
> The emotional complaints of our time, complaints we therapists hear every day in our practice, include
> - emptiness
> - meaninglessness
> - vague depression
> - disillusionment about marriage, family, and relationship
> - a loss of values
> - yearning for personal fulfillment
> - a hunger for spirituality
>
> All of these symptoms reflect a loss of soul and let us know what the soul craves.
> —Thomas Moore (xvi)

Liking someone means that in everyday life we have appreciation for the person and take time to be with and converse with the person. Love, as we so often understand it, permits us the privilege of relating to another abstractly—love them in our heart or love them in Christ or love them for what they can be. Jesus is talking about that abstract love and more. In the fellowship of the church, love includes the dimension of liking people. Liking people includes the disciplines of speaking to them, acknowledging them in public, and listening to what they say. Liking people is expressed as we commend them, as we do a favor for the person, buy them gifts, or permit the person to do a service for us. Liking a person will also include praying for him or her by name and allowing our relationship to grow, even at some personal risk.

Thomas Moore, author of the bestseller *Care of the Soul*, reminds us that "most, if not all, problems brought to therapists are issues of love," and the ultimate cure "is from love and not from logic" (Moore, 14). It is the cure that most—or all—of the members seek in the fellowship of the church.

5. Reconcile People

The church is in the reconciliation business. The term "to reconcile" in the English language means to compromise, acquiese, and mutually accept. The meaning suggested by Paul to the Corinthians is more precise: to be reconciled means to be brought into line, a correct relationship.

First we are reconciled with God. Our reconciliation is made possible because of Christ and then, as followers of Christ, we are given a message which seeks to reconcile persons to God. Our reconciliation with God includes caring relationships with persons in the local church (2 Corinthians 5:11—6:10), but goes beyond the fellowship with a task to reconcile persons who are estranged—couples, families, cultures, neighborhoods.

Freedom to forgive creates a community of God's people that becomes a model for reconciliation for the world. As the late Samuel Hines, pastor of the Third Street Church of God in Washington, DC, said:

The church must be the demonstration of unity—dogma divides but ministry unites. We need to create concrete examples of bridges between the estranged (Person to Person and Person to God). Christ commands this.

Highlighted are six reconciliation tasks identified by Sam, who was influential in reconciliation both locally and on a global scale. A practical note is sounded here, for we speak of a powerful idealism.

Reconciliation: Steps toward Change

1. We must recognize that the problem of estrangement exists and has damaging effects upon individuals and society.
2. We must take the responsibility for reducing estrangement rather than blaming each other.
3. We must take initiatives to solve the problems, rather than "seminaring" and "committeeing" ourselves to death.
4. We must repent, change our attitudes about ourselves, others, and life's situations.
5. We must, under God, direct our actions toward building loving relationships with one another and restoring justice and wholeness of life for all persons.
6. [We must] recognize that the commitment to change personally and in all human interactions is lifelong. The need for reconciliation will always be present. Reconciliation will not happen just because it is right. We must work at it continuously.

—Samuel G. Hines (29)

Reconciling people to God and each other is passionate ministry. It is possible, however, for it to be only a concept and discussed in classes and conferences.

Reconciliation has to be the practice of the church if it is to be the ministry of the church. If it will not work in the congregation of believers, then how in the world can it work anyplace else? To proclaim reconciliation and practice standoffishness is the height of hypocrisy.

By the same measure, reconciliation that is only practiced in the fellowship of the church and never reaches into the community is a sham. Reconciliation reaches out beyond the borders of the Christian fellowship to all human beings, of all types. Richard Foster, in his book on prayer, tells the following:

An elderly sage asked his followers, "How can we know when the darkness is leaving and the dawn is coming?"

One student said, "When we can see a tree in the distance and know that it is an elm and not a juniper."

Another said, "When we can see an animal and know that it is a fox and not a wolf."

The sage replied, "No, those things will not help us know."

"How then can we know?" the students asked.

The teacher drew himself up to full stature and replied, "We know the darkness is leaving and the dawn is coming when we can see another person and know that this is our brother or our sister; otherwise, no matter what time it is, it is still dark" (Foster, 249).

Reconciliation is not satisfied with darkness in divine or human relationships. Sin separates us from God and from other persons, sometimes from the persons whom we most love and whom we most need. It is only through grace that the restrictions and barriers of sin are removed. It is important that we talk about sin and grace at this point. Sin is universal but the grace of God encompasses everyone. Sin destroys people, and grace is a way out of sin. In the next chapter we will talk about how sin and divine grace relate to the people factor in the local church.

Ponder and Process

Action Process
Select three persons in your local fellowship about whom you know little and through conversation and observation seek to know them as persons.

Meditation Process
In what ways, and how, can you think more like a servant and serve persons who are members of your local church? How can you serve persons who live or work near you? Be very practical.

Discussion Process
Suggest that the group read 2 Corinthians 5:11–21. (In some groups one or more persons may not be acquainted with the contents of the Bible; therefore, give instructions, in a thoughtful way, on how to find the scripture portion.)

Ask the group to list areas of our lives that need reconciliation and ways persons in our community need to be reconciled to God and to one another.

Read the definition of *empathic listening* in this chapter. Give examples of times we are not listening at all, pretending to listen, practicing selective listening, and listening attentively.

Ask persons in the discussion group to tell of instances when they have listened, or been listened to, in one of these ways. Empathic listening, "listening with the intent to understand," is at another level. Ask the group to name persons who do empathic listening. What does empathic listening have to do with reconciliation?

Encourage group participants to pray personal prayers of confession about needs of reconciliation. Then ask them to pray for someone with whom they need to do a better job of listening. End the session with "The Lord bless you. Amen."

Chapter 3

THE SIN/GRACE FACTOR

We all need an understanding of sin. It is a part of our humanness and the Bible provides information about sin. If we talk about people we must talk about it. Sin is personal, but it has more than implications for an individual. We realize now more than ever the dimensions of remarks made by the brilliant atomic scientist J. Robert Oppenheimer. He said in 1947 to a group of scientists, "In some sort of crude sense, which no vulgarity, no humor, no overstatement can quite extinguish, the physicists have known sin, and this is a knowledge they cannot lose" (*Time*, 65). If we are concerned about people we will assist them as they deal with the problem of sin.

If we talk about sin, then we must eventually talk about grace, "God's unmerited free, spontaneous love for sinful man" (*Interpreter's Dictionary of the Bible*). Grace is incomprehensible, but one task of the church is to help people accept grace and live in grace. So, let us consider both subjects now.

Almost every news source in our world conveys bad news about sin. Here are some examples:

- Morning newspaper: In an Indianapolis local fast-food restaurant two robbers killed an elderly man and shot a young boy in the face.
- Magazine in my doctor's office: Millions of persons are paralyzed by alcohol and other drugs.
- Evening television news: An influential Chicago congressman has been convicted of misuse of funds and lost his powerful position in government and his participation in matters that could affect the lives of Americans for a century.
- A columnist writes: Hatred for persons of a different culture is resulting in the deaths of millions in eastern Europe, Central Africa, and South Africa. Missionary Robert Edwards says revenge is the enduring motive following the genocide that has taken the lives of more than a half-million persons in Rwanda.
- Television was saturated with the news of sports legend O. J. Simpson, who has a record of wife abuse and was the focus of unprecedented television and newspaper coverage during a trial in which he was accused of murder.

The sins of notorious persons get our attention on television and in the press, but sin is bad news also for persons whose names are not well known. Sin is bad news for those who sin and for the victims of their sin. Sin is, in fact, horrible news.

There is an exception. The Bible provides good news about sin. My wife and I often work the simpler crossword puzzles. I am positive that no clue for the word

Bible would ever be stated, "Good News about sin." Yet, it is one viable description.

The biblical writers were not naive; they knew that sin means spiritual death. They knew when one sins the harvest is guilt, destruction, and death. The prophet Hosea said what we have all learned about sin: "They sow the wind, and they shall reap the whirlwind" (8:7). The result of sin is always more than we bargain for.

Even so, the Bible has good news about sin.

Definition of Sin

Part of the good news is that the Bible defines sin, and in a world where sin seems to escape definition, that is helpful.

Those of us with a bent for philosophy and abstract theology enjoy inquiry into the origin and nature of sin. Those of us who have a taste for psychology repeatedly find ourselves exploring the causes of sin. Too often we conclude that the cause is outside ourselves, in the environment of the home or culture, and thus the sinner is really the victim. A conclusion like the following is difficult to avoid: in some respects sin is just a natural expression of our humanity. Everyone sins, so why be overly concerned?

In my mind and yours the question persists: What is sin anyway? What are we talking about? The Bible comes through with clear definitions and descriptions of sin. To begin with, the Ten Commandments give succinct statements about the foundations and explicit acts of sin:

- Worship God only—no one else and nothing else.

- Create no idols.
- Respect God's name and do not use God's name for flippant and selfish purposes.
- Set aside a day each week for worship and re-creation.
- Honor your parents.
- Do not murder, have adulterous affairs, steal, or lie.
- Do not think about obtaining what rightfully belongs to someone else by coveting (Exodus 20).

Some have objected that the Bible focuses on what one cannot do—the negative.

The Ten Commandments are worded in such a way that they can be read as negatives. Jesus helps us by summarizing the commandments with two positive statements:

"You shall love the Lord your God will all your heart, and with all your soul, and with all your mind." This is the greatest and first commandment. And a second is like it: "You shall love your neighbor as yourself" (Matthew 22:37–39).

Sin is more than a set of undesirable actions, according to Paul. He suggests that sin is a force that takes over one's life. Thus, he encourages the Roman Christians, in the name of Jesus Christ, to forbid sin to have power over their bodies (Romans 6:6 ff). No doubt about it, he is talking about the physical body, lest we tend to make the statement abstract.

The Apostle James explains that sin is giving in to temptation and desire (James 1:14) and then puts a twist on a definition of sin that has caused many of us to squirm: "Anyone, then, who knows the right thing to do, and fails to do it, commits sin" (James 4:17).

The Bible tells us that sin is living without God and failing to relate to other persons in caring and thoughtful ways. Many destructive acts are a part of our lives when God is left out and people are viewed as objects rather than personalities. To put it succinctly:

Sin is living without God at the center of life;
Sin is failing to respect persons.

Having defined what sin is, the New Testament repeatedly informs us that God has done something about our dilemma. Sin has a solution, sin has a cure.

> Since all have sinned and fall short of the glory of God; they are now justified by his grace as a gift, through the redemption that is in Christ Jesus (Romans 3:23–24; also 6:14).
>
> There is therefore now no condemnation for those who are in Christ Jesus. For the law of the Spirit of life in Christ Jesus has set you free from the law of sin and of death (Romans 8:1–2).

Sin is a persistent problem for all of us, even when we know what sin is and the lifestyle that God expects. Therefore, we need not only to know what sin is but also to understand more about the marvelous provision God has made to offset its effects in our lives—to remove us from the bondage of sin.

Forgiveness

Forgiveness is the wonderful news about sin.

Punishment is recommended as a cure for sin by most authorities. Fine and imprison, punish and restrict, are the preferred responses to all forms of sin. In practice, revenge is the reaction of choice—an eye for an eye, people say.

We are individually fearful of what might happen if our own sins were made public, though we may readily accept punishment as the best way to deal with the sins of other people. We may, therefore, deny wrongdoing and minimize our sinful attitudes. We find excuses for the ways we behave, the actions we take. Sin becomes something that society and other people have done to us. We recognize the feebleness of such a plea but it is an avenue for dealing with sin that all of us use.

Wrong actions, wrong attitudes, hurtful words, are some of the sins that cheapen our lives and destroy values that we cherish. The truth is, however, that no one can do anything about these destructive choices. That is the way the cookie crumbles. Everyone is helpless. That is the conclusion of parents, governments, and society.

The Bible is the exception. The Bible says that you and I can be forgiven, whatever the sin. We cannot live life over, and we cannot erase the past. Even so, sin can be forgiven—forgiven by God and, in turn, forgiven by one's self. A foundation is thus laid for seeking the forgiveness of persons who may have been the victims of our sin.

"When you sin," is an "even so" statement in the New Testament. Sin is a problem to persons who live without Christ but it may also become a problem for the sincere convert. Sin is an embarrassment to the follower of Jesus who has committed himself or herself to live in ways that honor God.

The Bible has good news about sin even when the Christian sins. The Apostle John explains it simply in one of his letters to the first-century churches:

> My little children, I am writing these things to you so that

> you may not sin. But if anyone does sin, we have an advocate with the Father, Jesus Christ the righteous; and he is the atoning sacrifice for our sins, and not for ours only but also for the sins of the whole world.
> (1 John 2:1–2)

This promise does not give us permission to do as we please, knowing full well that God has promised to forgive us in Christ. We are not to take seriously the quip, "It is easier to ask forgiveness than get permission." This scripture and similar ones in Paul's letter to the Romans can be misused as a license to sin. Paul faces the escapism issue head-on:

> What are we to say? Should we continue in sin in order that grace may abound? By no means! How can we who died to sin go on living in it?
> (Romans 6:1–2)

It is critically important that the believer hear the good news about sin, even though Paul challenges us to "walk in newness of life," to live without sin in our lives (Romans 6:4). The good news is that even Christians can be forgiven of their sins. Too many sincere followers of Christ fail to acknowledge sins in the first place and then live for years with a sense of guilt that confession and forgiveness can eradicate.

Our tendency is to deny sin, or justify sin through some rationale, to excuse attitudes and actions. We may say, "I am not the only one," or, "everyone else does too," or we think that nobody knows, so why be concerned?

We have an advocate in Jesus Christ and the forgiveness of sin for a Christian is the same as for any other person. Forgiveness comes as we confess and repent. The good news is that for anyone who sins there is forgiveness, even for the Christian that sins.

> **Sin Is Good News (?)**
> Sin is the best news there is, the best news there could be in our predicament.
> Because with sin, there's a way out. There's the possibility of repentance. You can't repent of confusion or psychological flaws inflicted by your parents—you're stuck with them. But you can repent of sin. Sin and repentance are the only grounds for hope and joy. The grounds for reconciled, joyful relationships. You can be born again.
> —John Alexander (36)

Grace

Grace is the experience that continues beyond initial forgiveness. It is at this very point that the devil robs many followers of Christ of a joyous life. Grace means that when we ask God for forgiveness in Christ, we are forgiven and that sin need no more plague us. We have acknowledged our sin and Christ has forgiven us. It is true others may have to work through accepting us if our sin has negatively affected their lives. That is not the point, however, when previously forgiven sins plague Christians.

Thousands of sincere, dedicated Christian believers suffer condemnation within themselves, and I believe from the devil, by failing to affirm the grace on which they stand. By grace a believer has repented and accepted forgiveness and need no longer be defeated by and harassed for past sins.

The good news for the Christian who is struggling with past sins is that grace takes care of the past relationships with God. The devil can no longer make it an issue, and the conscience is not free to revive painful memories.

> For there is no distinction, since all have sinned and fall short of the glory of God; they are now justified by his grace as a gift, through the redemption that is in Christ Jesus, whom God put forward as a sacrifice of atonement by his blood, effective through faith.
> (Romans 3:22b–25a)

His Grace, Not My Merit

Those who have the most difficult time extending grace to others are those who have the most difficult time receiving it for themselves (either because they don't think they really need it or they can't comprehend a God who would offer it).

I am sometimes confused by the strange mixture of shame (for my failures), wrongful pride (I'm better than some other people I know), doubt (will I ever have victory over my weaknesses), and grace (God knows my every flaw and loves me still) that envelops my soul. As I grow in Christ, it is His grace that overshadows the shame, the pride, and the doubt. It is His grace—not my merit—that gives me hope. It is the acceptance of His grace that makes me whole and sets the stage for victory over sin. As long as merit defines my heart, sin is inevitable. When grace overtakes me, holiness is within my grasp.

—Jim Lyon (1995)

The sin is forgiven! It is the good news that many Christians need to hear and accept for themselves so they can get on with life.

The farmer tells his banker that he has both good and bad news. The banker asks for the bad news first.

The farmer explains that because of the drought and

inflation he will not be able to pay a cent on the mortgage. Further, he will not be able to pay anything on the loan he had taken to buy machinery.

The banker is really fidgeting by this time and responds, "Boy, that is bad news!"

The farmer continues to remind the banker he had also borrowed money to buy seed and fertilizer and to take care of some living expenses, but he would not be able to pay a cent on that loan either.

The banker was obviously upset by this time and asked the farmer to tell him the good news.

The farmer explains, "The good news is that in spite of all this difficulty, I am going to continue doing business with you."

The farmer's confidence in the banker is like the trust a Christian can have in the grace of God. God will continue to be a loving parent who forgives. The privilege of repentance and confession are a part of God's grace. Christian, don't let the devil or your conscience rob you of the freedom that grace brings to you through Jesus Christ.

Recently I learned a grace-full story in the life of a dear friend in our local congregation, Nerine. Several years ago her son Keith had attended Anderson College but returned home for the summer and planned to continue his education at Michigan State University. One morning during breakfast with his mother he began to cry but did not let her know what was troubling him. He went to church camp that week and when he returned home he had a letter from his girlfriend.

Keith and his fiancée had purchased rings and were

to be married as soon as she was eighteen, in the fall. When his dad came home from work, Keith told him he was driving to Florida to get married but gave no reason for his decision. He drove straight through, finally stopping in Swainsboro, Georgia, to get a sandwich and gasoline. Soon after, he fell asleep at the wheel and collided head-on with an intoxicated driver. Keith died before his father and brother arrived. His mother was at a Christian Education Lab School and did not know of her son's accident until after his death. The state police found a letter in Keith's car that had informed him that his girl friend was pregnant.

Nerine and her husband invited Keith's fiancée to the memorial service and she sat with the family. When they had learned she was pregnant with their first grandchild, they felt they had some responsibility for her and the baby—sustaining Keith's love and responsibility. They sought legal advice and it was agreed that the young woman and the baby would take the family's name. She came to live with the family and the baby was born the next January. Within eighteen months the young mother met a fine young man, and they were married. They had five children and Nerine and her husband have made them their grandchildren, "with no distinctions made."

This family expressed grace. It was undeserved, unexpected, totally beautiful, loving, magnificently liberating. So is the grace that God offers us.

Power

God provides power for victory over sin and that is good news. The Holy Spirit indwells a believer, cleanses the person's life, gives power over temptation, and provides a greater purpose for living.

Added to all God will do for a person through the Holy Spirit is the call for the person to decide to use his or her own power. We cannot prevent sin but if our will is harnessed with the power of the Spirit we can have victory over sin.

> Therefore, do not let sin exercise dominion in your mortal bodies, to make you obey their passions. No longer present your members to sin as instruments of wickedness, but present yourselves to God as those who have been brought from death to life, and present your members to God as instruments of righteousness.
>
> For sin will have no dominion over you, since you are not under law but under grace.
>
> (Romans 6:12–14)

Good news! Your life is no longer as it was when sin had control. When one accepts Christ the power of sin is history. The power of sin is buried. Now in Christ every forgiven person who has accepted Christ as Savior can say, "I can do all things through him who gives me strength" (Philippians 4:13).

It is because of Christ that the believer can accept the challenge that Paul gave the Roman Christians:

> I appeal to you therefore, brothers and sisters, by the mercies of God, to present your bodies as a living sacrifice, holy and acceptable to God, which is your spiritual worship. Do not be conformed to this world, but be transformed by the renewing of your minds, so that you may discern what is the will of God—what is good and acceptable and perfect.
>
> (Romans 12:1–2)

Power for righteousness and power over sin is provided through:

- prayer,
- the community of believers,
- special persons like pastors,
- the scriptures, and
- our own decision to follow Christ.

Most of all a saving relationship with God in Christ gives a person power over sin.

Laura and I have traveled in parts of Pennsylvania, Ohio, and Indiana where we have occasionally observed very lovely farmhouses that for some reason did not look quite right to us. Something was different. After a while we would figure out what was different. No power lines. Clothes were hanging on the lines to dry. No antennas for television or radio.

We would soon realize these were Amish homes and would be reminded of the depth and sincerity of their beliefs and practice of the faith. One cannot but regret that they have not tapped into a power that can bring so much joy and freedom to a home, if used with discipline. Electrical power could bring blessings to the home that would lighten workloads and provide many physical comforts.

Many Christians let another power, the power for righteous living, go untapped.

Contact with God in worship, in confession, in seeking the mind of Christ all bring power to the Christian. Power has to be tapped, contact retained, and supply lines kept connected. Power is available to live with victory over sin.

A rather reserved and traditional bishop became acquainted with a woman in his charge who had more of a charismatic leaning. She repeatedly came to him with reports of recent conversations with Jesus. After several fruitless attempts to help the woman get her experiences in proper perspective the bishop had an idea he thought would end her hallucinations. He explained to her, "Two weeks ago I confessed to Jesus a sin I had never confessed before and which had bothered me for years. The next time Jesus appears to you ask him what the sin was that I confessed two weeks ago." The woman thought it was a reasonable request.

Several weeks later she returned to the bishop's office and announced that Jesus had again appeared to her. The bishop reminded her of his instruction to ask Jesus about the sin he had confessed. She replied, "Oh yes, I asked him if he remembered that sin. He said that he remembered your confession but couldn't remember the sin at all." That is what grace does with sin!

Every person in every congregation must deal with the problem of sin. Every person in every congregation relies on the grace of God for forgiveness and power. There are no exceptions. When the good news about sin and grace are understood and appropriated into people's lives, the church goes a long way toward becoming the redemptive fellowship it is intended to be.

Illness and suffering are also a part of the human existence and none escape the hurts and limitations that come with pain. The illness may be physical, mental, emotional, or relational but the suffering person seeks healing in some way. The church has prayer and healing as a part of its ministry to people, and it is to this ministry we will now speak.

Ponder and Process

Action Process

Forgive a member of your family or a friend. Pray for a willingness and a strength to forgive. If appropriate and if it would be helpful, let the other person know you have forgiven. Ask for his or her forgiveness in return.

Meditation Process

Consider the sins for which God has forgiven you. Contemplate the richness in your life as a result of the free gift of God's love.

Discussion Process

Ask five members of the group to read one of the following scriptures from Romans: 3:21–25; 6:1–4; 6:12–14; 8:1–5; and 12:1–2. The leader may summarize definitions of sin provided in this chapter and give opportunity for the group to add their understandings of sin.

Identify with the group ways we attempt to earn God's love and forgiveness.

Consider in conversation what ways we have power over sin. Discuss ways we are vulnerable to temptation as long as we live.

Pose the question, What does it mean to "walk in newness of life?" Ask if there is a person in the group who has **not** accepted forgiveness of sin and is not living in Christ. The concluding prayer could be a prayer of repentance with a member of the group.

Pray in unison or ask one person to read:

> Dear Lord and Father of mankind,
> forgive our foolish ways!
> Reclothe us in our rightful mind;
> In purer lives thy service find,
> In deeper reverence, praise. Amen.
>
> —John Greenleaf Whittier

Chapter 4

THE ILLNESS/HEALING FACTOR

I was embarrassed when I realized what I had done. A telephone call to the Riverchase South Church in Birmingham let the lay leaders know that I would not be with them the next weekend to speak and meet with their Elders. The previous Sunday I had met with them but that evening had become extremely ill and had not recovered a stable stomach or energy. They knew I had been ill and were gracious in excusing me. After I telephoned I remembered that I was planning to speak on divine healing. Embarrassing!

Much that goes under the claim of divine healing is embarrassing today. Some television personalities make healing a theatrical production. Others make claims about persons being healed, but a casual follow-up reveals the claims as false. An informed pastor told me one healer said that six had been totally cured of cancer, though contacts six months later revealed all those "totally healed" had died. For the most part, that which gets the greatest exposure as divine healing in our generation is not divine, is not healing, and diverts the church from a valid focus on healing.

People participating in the life of the local congregation are in need of healing. It is not some people or a few people or an occasional person. People are hurting in a variety of ways, but they all are hurting, sometime and in some way. It is, therefore, absolutely necessary that a church discover ways to minister to suffering people through prayer, biblically based counseling, and correct teaching on the whole subject of divine healing.

Divine healing as a result of prayer is included in the promises of the New Testament. Problems may occur, however, in our minds and our religious experiences when we assume that the prayer of faith will immediately bring healing for every illness and every disease. Psalm 103 is often quoted as assurance of healing and has caused some to believe that Christians may expect cures for any illness from which they pray for relief, if they have faith:

> Bless the LORD, O my soul, and all that is within me,
>   bless his holy name.
> Bless the LORD, O my soul, and do not forget all his
>   benefits—
> who forgives all your iniquity,
> who heals all your diseases.
>
> (vv 1, 3b)

Within my church fellowship we have heard leading ministers strongly state it is the Lord's will to heal all diseases. A dear friend, Maurice Berquest, often preached from this text. He suggested, at least as I understood him, that God chooses to heal those of us who suffer, and it is a matter of appropriately aligning one's will and spirit with his to experience healing and health. Berk, as we knew him, was unusually intelligent, deeply spiritual in the best sense of the term, and a convincing preacher. Even so, many of us are not persuaded that healing is as totally encompassing as many honest Christians and a number of less reputable healers insist. We find ourselves questing for truth with persons like Berk and having little in common with those who appear to have ulterior motives for expressing their healing theologies.

A quick study of a set of scriptures fits well into the presentations of those who suggest it is God's will that everyone be healed. A look at chapters eight, nine, and ten of Matthew's Gospel may be helpful:

> *Matthew 9:18–26:* A man asks Jesus to come heal his daughter; on the way a woman with a hemorrhage touches his cloak and is healed. Also, Matthew 14:36 tells of a woman who touched the "fringe of his cloak" and was healed.
>
> *27–31:* Jesus healed two blind men, "according to your faith."
>
> *32–34:* Jesus healed a demoniac who is mute.
>
> *35–36:* Jesus' continuing ministry is described, and it includes a phrase: "curing every disease and every sickness."
>
> *Matthew 10:1:* Jesus commissioned the twelve disciples and gave the "authority over unclean spirits, to cast them out, and to cure every disease and every sickness."
>
> *Matthew 8:16:* After healing the mother-in-law of Peter of a fever, Jesus cast out demons and "cured all who were sick."

Perhaps that portion of what is recorded in the New Testament is hyperbole, an exaggeration for emphasis. Therefore, terms translated "all" and "every" may have been expressions of awe more than a statistical report. Nonetheless, the reports are eyewitness accounts and we do not have the privilege of adjusting them much for language or culture, in a rewrite of history. It is true that the record is made by a human being who is himself awestruck by the person and ministry of Jesus, and in such a state we could presume it honestly looked to the writer as though everyone were being healed of everything.

The scriptures give us a clue that not all diseases were cured; we know only one resurrected human by name, Lazarus, and not everyone was healed. For instance, Jesus was hindered in Nazareth "because of their unbelief," an unbelief that was outright opposition to Jesus (Matthew 13:54–58). The disciples were asked to heal an epileptic boy whose seizures were so severe that he sometimes rolled into fire or water. They could not do it, and when they asked Jesus the reason, he explained it was their lack of faith. Notice it was not related to the amount of faith, for he said all that was needed was comparable to a mustard seed, a very small seed. We are left to wonder: was it because they had come to believe some power resided in them and they were using the formulas and neglecting the divine mystery? (Matthew 17:14–21).

One more: 2 Corinthians 12:8 records that the Apostle Paul prayed for healing for himself, and we may presume he had enlisted others to pray for him, but he was not healed. Out of his experience comes the wonderfully reassuring phrase, "My grace is sufficient for you, for power is made perfect in weakness."

It is my opinion that healing, this wonderful teaching and belief of the church, is being overdone by television healers; they stretch credulity, often their cute theatrics bring disdain for the cause of Christ, and too often their ministries seem to be geared to abnormal quests for finances and ostentatious lifestyles. Healing and wealth are often paired, and the suggestion is that health and material possessions indicate God's approval on one's life and thus bring happiness. They have overemphasized the physical healing aspect of the gospel; I believe the gospel focuses more on the need to be healed of sin, and sin is the ultimate disease from which God seeks to save us.

In the church I attend we underemphasize healing. No doubt part of our hesitance to encourage prayers for healing is our desire to avoid the excesses of some healers. We are wise to do so, for we must critique those who highlight the promises of God and rarely speak of discipleship, giving up all to follow Jesus wherever and whenever. Promises sell better than responsibility.

However, healing is a part of the message of the gospel for us. In addition to healing from the curse and power of sin, we are also encouraged to seek healing for physical and other illnesses in our lives. The Bible and history of the church lead us to no other conclusion.

Need for Healing

Many persons need divine healing. They need a special divine intervention, for their condition is desperate, and they are suffering without relief. We have been granted the privilege by our Lord and by the scriptures of praying for anything we need. That includes physical healing, and we need not be reticent about it. Medicine and surgery are among the ways God has blessed our generation with healing opportunities, and the answer to many of our prayers for health are answered through medical science; my inherited cardiac and blood pressure problems are graciously controlled by medicines.

Many persons suffer intensely in ways that are not physical but probably have implications for the physical body. Persons are suffering

- from experiences that have negatively affected their self-esteem;
- from estranged or uncomfortable relationships;
- from unredeemed attitudes;
- from the inability to accept normal experiences of life such as change.

These conditions often result in bitterness, anger, and strife, and persons are not able to break the pattern of inner suffering and dysfunction that are a result of these emotional cancers. Some persons become reclusive, that is, they retreat into a protective shell and lose, thereby, a significant part of their lives. These people suffer emotionally, socially, and physically. It is difficult for physicians, counselors, pastors, and friends to distinguish between what are the emotional, spiritual, and physical factors in a person's illness. Nearly all scientific and religious disciplines see a close correlation between an illness and all other aspects of a person's life.

Earlier I mentioned the stomach illness that caused me to cancel a speaking engagement in Birmingham.

That week in a conversation with my wife, we both observed that occasionally a physical illness may cause us to slow down in order for our spirit and mind to be healed—healed from overscheduling and overobligating ourselves. Thus, we thought, my physical discomfort may have enabled a deeper and more needed healing in my lifestyle.

Why is it important to say this? Is this not a way of discouraging persons who only know they are hurting and are crying out for help? It is important to say this because many persons who are hurting are not going to be helped much by divine removal of a physical disease (obviously many would be). It is necessary any time we consider prayer and divine healing that we pray for what we want, identify how we hurt, but open ourselves to be healed where we need healing most.

If our attitudes, therefore, desperately need to be healed, maybe a prayer for our attitude would relieve corresponding physical ailments. It is probable that attention to spiritual healing, including a correct knowledge of the grace of God and forgiveness, could make one's physical suffering endurable. Again, physical suffering is so painful for some that it may seem uncaring to even suggest this. To be sure, I pray for anyone who requests prayer and I believe that God finds many ways to heal persons. What I am emphasizing is that we are healed most completely when we permit God to heal us where we need it the most and where it will do the most good. The healing often most needed is in our spiritual understanding and our emotional experiences.

Normal Experiences

If we attempt to avoid the normal experiences of life through prayer for healing, then we are asking too much. We can find strength to cope with life through the scriptures, prayer, and worship with believers. Some of the normal experiences of life are

• *Sickness which is common to everyone*; for instance the common cold, for most of us will last about four days, I am told, and then it will get better. What we do is take medicine to help us endure and keep us quiet enough for others to endure us. The common cold is horrible, but it is not a personal attack by God or the devil on any of us. It is just a part of being alive.

• *Limited ability* is normal; we are all finite but our finiteness is expressed in different persons in different ways. The chafing at limited ability may take the form of resentment or in expressions such as "life is not fair." Restricted function—physical and, perhaps in some, mental and social—becomes more noticeable for many persons as they age. These restrictions are not something we need to be healed from; they are placed before God, believing God will be with us in every experience of life.

• *Death* is a normal experience, a nearly universal experience, with the exception of those who have the Enoch provisions in their contract. Enoch walked with God and then was not (Genesis 5:24). We are made to grasp life but we are not going to be healed from death; it is going to happen and that is not bad.

• *Hurt by others* is normal; often this takes the form of betrayal. We tend to write scripts in our mind and our expectations are that other persons will follow our scripts, and when they do not, we are hurt by the way they have "betrayed" our expectations. Also, some persons intend to hurt us. They may hurt others because of something they have experienced, a misunderstanding, or a habit they have. Whatever the reason, being hurt by other persons is a normal experience.

• *Decisions will be regretted.* Words and deeds fit into that category, too. Decisions are made with available information and days or years later we may have additional information or a different attitude and thus regret a decision. We acknowledge wise decisions are based on wide considerations of options and prayer, but even so we will regret at least a few decisions, and that is normal.

Do not be defeated or destroyed by common occurrences of life. Furthermore, accept many experiences as normal, and do not spend undue time attempting to persuade God to save you from that which is part of being alive. Jesus was not liked by everyone, for instance, and probably God is not overly concerned when our living quarters are not luxurious when many others of his children are homeless.

Divine Healing

When we pray for divine healing we affirm that the healing we all need most is salvation from sin and a hope for eternal life with Christ. Divine healing is a phrase we use to talk about God's deliverance from complicated miseries and suffering in life. Most often we think of divine healing in regard to physical suffering or illnesses. Let us look beyond that limited view to discover what the scriptures and church history have taught us.

Divine healing includes the following:

Physical healing—as a result of prayer and faith a person is cured of a physical ailment, in what way and to what extent we have never understood.

Psychic healing involves the healing of emotions, better information about God and life, and attitudinal changes—all as a result of prayer and the special intervention of God in one's life.

Demonic healing has at least two aspects. Sin may be coloring the experiences of life because we permit it to do so. Demonic possession is a different thing—it is the power of evil in our lives even though we do not want it to be there. It may be the demon is a spirit that has a voice and personality of its own, though I confess I have never encountered such a demon.

It may be a demon that is inflicted by curses such as "You are mean," "You are lazy," "You are no account," "You are ugly," or a thousand thoughtless curses that have embedded themselves in our unconscious because someone spoke them to us.

Cultural healing is needed in some of our lives. Our culture has wrong concepts about material possessions; about young being beautiful and old being undesirable; about violence being an acceptable pattern for handling differences; about God helping those who help themselves (a quotation from Ben Franklin reportedly identified by more Americans as a favorite scripture than any other quote); about some kinds of people being better than other kinds (race and gender); and abnormal stress being accepted as normal. Many of us need cultural healing.

Something more needs to be said about demonic

spirits that afflict so many and from which there seems little hope of release outside of the healing touch of God.

> **Stress**
> Stress becomes distress when for any reason we begin to sense a loss of our feelings of security and adequacy.... Helplessness, desperation, and disappointment turn stress into distress. Distress is the stress of losing.
> —Karl Albrecht (61)
> Anything—pleasant or unpleasant—that arouses your adrenaline system and mobilizes your body for "fight or flight," then doesn't let up and allow time for recovery, can predispose you to stress disease. Your body simply adapts to living in a constant state of emergency—and you feel no discomfort until damaging results occur.
> —Archibald D. Hart (30)

• *Family problems* of years ago are lived and relived with persons feeling possessed and dominated by the problem; strife in the home, for instance, remains a factor in everyday life though experienced years ago as a child or teen.

• *Family traits or cultural traditions* are so ingrained that a person cannot seem to escape them, for instance racial prejudice, explosiveness, distrust of most people.

• *A curse,* as mentioned above, can be words spoken casually or intentionally that have repeatedly caused unhappiness; even sexual molestation, brutality, verbal abuse are among those curses with which some have to live.

• *Carryover from a former style of life*—the demons, as it were, still haunt—such as adulterous life, war, alcohol, drugs, stinginess.

- *Antisocial behavior* may be wild, unpredictable, destructive.
- *Habits, addictions*—several ways are available to help persons escape these demonic powers, but the power of prayer added to other sources is absolutely necessary for genuine healing to take place.

Just thinking right is not enough. Most of us have worked at thinking positively, thinking correctly, and attempting to think like Jesus, all very desirable efforts. Prayer and the touch of God are needed to bring about the healing needed.

Steps of Prayer for Healing

James 5:13–16 is an excellent scriptural reference point for prayer, faith, and healing:

1. It is a precise and succinct statement about praying for those who are ill.
2. It tells the afflicted person to call the elders.
3. It provides a simple procedure or formula—anoint with oil, pray the prayer of faith, in the name of the Lord—with the promise: healing.
4. It also emphatically relates physical healing to other aspects or experiences of one's life—the person is instructed to identify unconfessed sin. The connection between physical, emotional, or mental, and the spiritual is strongly affirmed and the scriptures leave no doubt but that the most important is healing from sin.

Lest the latter be overstated, understand that this scripture is not saying, "You are sick and so you must have sin in your life." Rather, it is recognizing what every investigation into the quality of human life has discovered: to have health we must consider all compartments of our lives, especially attitudes and lifestyle. This instruction is not meant to dissuade us from requesting prayer. Quite the contrary, it encourages those of us who are ill to seek prayer. James is being very fair to us as we would want any doctor or counselor to be. He is saying, "Let us look closely at your situation to make sure we are praying about the right thing."

> **James 5:13–16**
> Are any among you suffering? They should pray. Are any cheerful? They should sing songs of praise. Are any among you sick? They should call for the elders of the church and have them pray over them, anointing them with oil in the name of the Lord. The prayer of faith will save the sick, and the Lord will raise them up; and anyone who has committed sins will be forgiven. Therefore confess your sins to one another, and pray for one another, so that you may be healed. The prayer of the righteous is powerful and effective.

We rely on the scriptures but also the experience of those who have prayed for persons who are ill. We know that when we anoint persons, often we anoint them in anticipation that some other action will enable healing, such as surgery. We anoint persons sometimes in a type of proxy as they request prayer for someone meaningful to them, similar to Paul's use of handkerchiefs (Acts 19:12). When we pray for each other at the point of our need, it is wise to follow some simple guidelines in addition to the biblical formula provided by James.

Guidelines for Anointing and Prayer

1. *Assess* the situation of the person and the illness before praying. This is a factor often neglected, therefore, more attention will be focused on discerning needs beyond the acknowledged illness than on the other guidelines. Adequate assessment is not always possible in the brief time we allow for prayer in public worship services. Make some assessment in private conversations before prayer. As you assess the need be aware that an abundance of grace, comfort, and healing are already available.

I've had the privilege of staying in the home of friends as I have traveled. On occasion it is necessary to be in their home alone for an extended period of time. More than once I have been told by a host that would be absent during the day, "You can have anything you want in the refrigerator; the cereal is in the cupboard." Similarly, God has made some blessings available to us on request. The Bible, personal and private times of prayer and meditation, fellowship with Christians, confession of guilt or fear, and guidance through the counseling of a respected and trusted fellow Christian are all made available to us whenever we want them. These ministries to our suffering are available on request; just take them.

When a person requests to be anointed and prayed for, the "elders" need to listen carefully. The gift of discernment is important—perceiving possible causes for an illness beyond the obvious physical symptoms. The person is probably asking for prayer for a particular illness, and it is appropriate to pray for that felt need. It is also important to listen to what else is being communicated. You may discern additional information during the conversation, perhaps an unresolved hurt. You may know the person's history and be aware of experiences or habits that contribute to ill health. The Holy Spirit may impress on your mind an insight or a caring curiosity about memories that may be hindering a healthful lifestyle. Spiritual and psychological suffering produce physical illnesses; sometimes persons need assistance in recognizing and dealing with inner feelings that are contributing to illness.

In the summer of 1995 Laura and I enjoyed being guests for the Minnesota Church of God Camp Meeting. One evening I spoke on divine healing and invited persons to come to the front of the worship center and request prayer by pastors and lay leaders. A lovely couple, probably still in their twenties, and their two sons were among the campers. The woman knelt at an altar and when a pastor spoke with her she asked to be healed of her shyness, something she felt was a great restriction on her life.

The pastor immediately prayed and asked the Lord to heal her sinuses.

The woman hesitated a minute and then told the pastor that her problem was shyness. He inquired whether it caused her headaches and then in a moment proceeded to pray again that her sinuses would be healed.

Rather desperate (perhaps her shyness was put to the ultimate test) she again explained to the pastor that her problem was shyness and not sinuses. The next day the pastor who prayed for her was a bit shy about telling the story but laughed with us about his mistake.

The Illness/Healing Factor

Someone said, in jest of course, that the woman's sinuses had never been so clear.

A degree of boldness in thoughtful and kindly inquiry could improve our prayer ministries. It may be a word that prompts the individual to search a bit further. We may pursue impressions as long as we can honestly say that we are attempting to help the person. Pursuit of information to satisfy personal curiosity is not valid or ethical.

One error we make is to pray for a surgical procedure, for instance, when actually we could be more helpfully praying with persons about their fears—fear of hurting, fear of loneliness, fear of death. Healing of the fears may be more far reaching than the experience of health for which the prayer was originally requested. Other prayer needs involve repressed guilt, deep-seated bitterness, unacknowledged hurts, and uncomfortable relationships.

When we can help ourselves be honest about our own needs when we are suffering, and when we can help others be honest about what is really troubling them and making them ill, then real healing can take place.

For instance, Jim is in the hospital. He is going to have heart surgery and, though he is a person who has feared nothing in life, he is obviously totally fearful now. The pastor and two men from the church anoint Jim and pray for him. The pastor senses a need for something more and tells the other two he will join them in a minute so that he can speak with Jim alone. The pastor explains to Jim that he feels something else is wrong and inquires if he might help. Jim confesses, "Quite frankly, pastor, I have been a part of the church for years, but if I don't come off that operating table alive, I think I will probably go to hell; not a pleasant thought." The pastor explained the simple gospel message for making things right with God: confession of sin, acceptance of forgiveness, and a commitment to Jesus Christ as Savior and Lord. The pastor added some explanation of God's love and grace toward Jim. Then the pastor prayed. Jim was healed in a way he most needed healing—healed of sin and healed of fear. He went into surgery with a sense of peace, as he later explained, even though he still didn't like undergoing surgery.

It is appropriate for the "elder" who is counseling with the person seeking prayer to suggest she or he might consider other needs. It is not the task of the counselor, however, to probe for causes the person does not want to discuss. The prayer for healing can always include an entreaty that each person be open to all the healing God wants to give us.

2. Ask God for healing. James 5:13–16 instructs us to pray for healing. Jesus said in a comprehensive way, "Ask and you will receive, so that your joy may be complete" (John 16:24). Even more emphatically, "Whatever you ask for in prayer, believe that you have received it, and it will be yours" (Mark 11:24).

Maxie Dunham, Methodist pastor now president of Asbury Seminary, confesses he readily prayed for deliverance from pain, "strength to be," guidance for doctors, and support for loved ones but not for outright healing. He points to the scriptures and encourages us to be specific in our prayers (*The Workbook of Intercessory Prayer*, 23–25). We are also tempted to persuade God to heal, or provide God with excuses in case God does not want to do as we request. It is not our role, however, to list easy outs for God. We pray for what we want but our trust is in a God who loves us and wants the best for each of us.

The Doctor Prays

The devil tries to kill them with his dreadful arsenal: tumors, aneurysms, strokes, traumas. Dr. Overton, at age 59 a veteran of more than 4,000 operations, takes up his instruments and applies his vast knowledge of the brain's circuitry to keeping his patients alive. But he knows that it isn't up to him to save them: He sometimes asks patients scheduled for surgery, "If something goes wrong, are you comfortable that you know God and you'll go to heaven?"

Some patients switch doctors when they hear him ask that, and Dr. Overton understands. He himself was once a skeptic.

—*Wall Street Journal* (A1)

---

3. *Assume that God will not only do what is best* but also will keep promises. Something good happens when a human being presents himself or herself before God and requests help at a point of need. One person was told that answers to prayer were coincidences, to which he responded, "All I know is that I have a lot more coincidences when I pray than when I don't."

Some months ago Laura was asked by our granddaughter Brianna for a Popsicle at 9 A.M. Laura thought it a bit early for that type of snack but suggested some cereal she knew Brianna likes. At lunch she gave Brianna additional nourishing and tasty food. For an afternoon snack she offered the Popsicle. Seems sensible doesn't it? God is like that. God knows what his children need and thoroughly enjoys relating to them, often giving them specifically what they ask for, but wanting to give them much more than they ever knew to ask for. Jesus encourages us to ask and adds this:

> If you then, who are evil, know how to give good gifts to your children, how much more will your Father in heaven give good things to those who ask him!
> (Matthew 7:11)

4. *Accept the promises of God.* Accept the action of God. Accept the presence of God. Healing is often discovered in the acceptance that God is with us as Creator, as sustainer, as Savior and Lord, and in the present ministry of the Holy Spirit—right here and right now.

Most of all, persons who are seeking healing may need to be reminded to accept the forgiveness that God has given and to forgive themselves.

Healing Services

Persons who wish to be anointed or have hands laid on them for prayer are invited to come to the altar of my home congregation each Sunday morning. It is a very meaningful time for those facing surgery, a move, grief, or other stressful times. When I was a pastor in Casper, Wyoming, I continued a practice started by my predecessor Calvin Brallier. Persons who wished to be anointed with oil (James 5:13–16) were asked to stand at the altar before the pastoral prayer was offered, express quietly and succinctly their concern, and to be assured that the pastors joined them in prayer for their concern. The concerns expressed were often for other persons and for needs other than physical—emotional and relational healings were a part of the prayer requests.

As the congregation grew, persons lined up to be anointed on Sunday mornings. At times two or three pastors were at the head of lines of people waiting to be anointed. We did not do that every Sunday, for there were other elements of worship that were important to the total congregation. It was, however, a practice that benefited our people who needed a special touch from God. Persons also were anointed and prayed for in other services when they requested it, in the hospital, and by appointment. These methods of praying for persons with physical, emotional, economic, relational, and other needs are valid.

Another suggested model: Once a week, or once a month—perhaps on a weekday night or Saturday—have a Prayer-for-Healing Service. The service would be low key, that is, not highly dramatic, avoiding attempts to hypnotize the congregation with voice or music. Sing hymns and thoughtful choruses with, perhaps, a solo in a meditative mode. The pastor could bring a brief and simple exposition on a relevant scripture.

Persons would then be invited to come to the front of the room or sanctuary for anointing and prayer. The seekers would be instructed to kneel at an altar or sit on the front row of seats. A prayer counselor would join each person who comes forward and the seeker would be encouraged to speak honestly and specifically about his or her need for healing. Persons might also seek anointing and prayer in behalf of another.

Counselors should use guidelines such as those suggested earlier in this chapter, and be enlisted and trained by the pastor or a similarly qualified leader in the church. It is also important that participants be familiar with the nature of the church's teaching on healing. Avoid letting undisciplined persons oversimplify or abort the marvelous process of prayer for healing.

Following the guidelines, prayer counselors would be enabled to learn and discern the needs that the seeker may or may not be aware of and pray for healings that may be beyond the scope of the initial request.

The service probably should go no longer than one hour, and it is not necessary to attract large crowds. This is a ministry to persons who are suffering and who earnestly seek prayer for themselves or for ones they love.

I wish I had done this when I was pastor. I am indebted to my mentor John T. Finney who experimented with this idea in Nottingham, England, and found the church crowded the second week the healing service was convened.

The surprise that a congregation experiences is rewarding. Most persons know that everyone is not going to be healed—they are aware of the reasons we have mentioned above. But healing does happen and in marvelous ways. Fred Craddock, a teacher of preachers at Emory University, tells a humorous story that illustrates the surprise that could come to our churches:

A pastor visited an elderly woman who was near death, in a pitiful condition. He asked if there were anything she would like for him to do for her. She whispered that she would like for him to pray. He asked if she had something specific in mind and she said, "I would like for you to pray for my healing, of course." He hesitated, but then prayed that if it were in keeping with God's will her request be granted and if not, then everyone would adjust to the situation. He closed with "Amen."

The woman sat up in bed and exclaimed, "Wow!" She jumped out of bed, stood up, flexed her muscles, and said, "This is unbelievable! I feel wonderful." She walked down the hall and told the nurses, "I think I'm well! I think I'm well!"

The pastor left the hospital in shock and got into his car. There upon he said, "God, don't you ever do that to me again."

We continue to be surprised when God specifically answers our prayers.

Ponder and Process

Action Process
Speak with your pastor and lay leaders about interest in having a service in which persons are anointed and prayed for.

Meditation Process
Do you have hesitations to pray for physical, mental, emotional, or relationship needs in your life. Why?

Discussion Process
List ways stress affects our physical and mental health. Can it also affect our spiritual lives?

Ask one person (preferably beforehand) to relate a story of healing that has taken place in the past two years. Ask, "If any of you in this group were to seek prayer for divine healing, what need would you identify?" Consider, "Would it be appropriate for us to anoint each other and pray now?"

Identify three healings that your group would most like to realize in the fellowship of your congregation—the healings may be physical, emotional, relational, whatever. Agree in prayer for these three healings. Make a note to ask for reports on how healings are taking place.

Chapter 5

THE VOCATION FACTOR

At one time or another most Christians struggle with questions related to vocation—divine call or appointment. Specifically:
• Does God create us for, and call us to, very specific tasks or ministries?
• Or is the call a more general one and each of us is free to respond in our own way to God's call?

Is God's call individual, personal and unique? Is God's call to any and all who will respond and in ways they may choose?

The answer is *Yes!* The call of God on our lives is specific and in general. It is with that dual experience of divine call that many of us need help. The answer, however, may be more troubling than the question if left as only a yes. When I was eighteen years old I thought I would resolve that question in a year or two, undoubtedly before college graduation. However, it persists for me today and sometimes in a more troubling dimension. Not only do I now consider the future, but I evaluate the past as I think about my divine call—vocation.

In my teen years I was quite sure that I could handle anything God wanted me to do. Now I am not quite so confident.

I know how much courage it takes to follow the leading of the Lord. I know something of the sacrifice. I know something of the pain. To be sure, I also know much about the pleasure, the joy, the reward, and the satisfaction that come from doing the will of the Lord. Even so, I now know that following the Lord's will for my life is risky and I now insist on more information than I would have requested in former years. Moses was called to lead the Jewish people out of slavery in Egypt when he was an old man and apparently comfortable in his lifestyle. God spoke to him out of a burning bush, and Moses was puzzled by the call. He insisted God was making a mistake and offered alternatives (Exodus 3 and 4). As an adult the matter of divine call is still a mysterious dynamic in my life. The assignments God seems to have for me are puzzling at times, though mine are on a far smaller scale than those of Moses and others whose names we will mention.

Chosen from Birth

First, let us acknowledge that at least some appear to have been chosen for a specific task from the time of birth. Samuel was dedicated to the Lord's work even before he was conceived, and his mother Hannah presented him as a boy saying,

For this child I prayed; and the LORD has granted me the petition that I made to him. Therefore I have lent him to the LORD; as long as he lives, he is given to the LORD.
(1 Samuel 1:27–28)

Jeremiah is even more specific about a prenatal divine assignment:

Now the word of the LORD came to me saying,
"Before I formed you in the womb I knew you,
and before you were born I consecrated you;
I appointed you a prophet to the nations."
(Jeremiah 1:4–5)

John the Baptist and Jesus also had assignments before they were born (Luke 1). The biblical record and history strongly indicate that at least some persons are brought into existence for a particular assignment. In recent history persons like Gandhi and Martin Luther King, Jr. seem to have been persons of destiny; perhaps we shall one day say that of Billy Graham, too.

Though we acknowledge that at least some persons have a divine assignment from birth, even the biblical record and certainly history leave us with doubt that everyone is so identified and prepared from birth. Many mothers, and some fathers, believe their children to be persons of destiny. You have heard the oft-told tale by Jewish comedians about the mother who introduced her two-year-old and four-year-old children as "my son the doctor and my son the lawyer."

It is not necessary that we pursue the enigma of personal destiny from birth; we cannot find all the answers. The puzzle between the other two options, the general will of God for our lives and the specific will of God for our lives, is our focus and continues to be important, whatever our age.

The General Will of God

A concept of the general will of God may be expressed in several ways, but let us do it in this simple form:

God expects us to love him and love people. We have freedom to serve God and serve our fellow human beings in any place and in any ways we choose.

It could be said that this is the "bloom where you are planted" theory of divine leadership in our lives. At least twice in my past when I was attempting to make a decision about my ministry, persons whom I greatly respected said, "Oral, God doesn't want you more in one place than he does any other. God just expects you to serve him wherever you are."

Generally all persons are called to repent and be baptized, to follow the Lord's teachings, to worship, to be profitable stewards, to be generous, and to live lives set apart for God—holy lives. If each of us were committed to do that, undoubtedly we would realize the victory of God in our world, in our homes, and in our churches. We may on the basis of scripture and experience be assured that God has a general plan for all of us, for each of us.

Specific Will of God

What about the idea of a more specific call?

God has a specific assignment for us and will at times be adjusting the assignment and may change the place where we are to serve.

The call of God is often specific as to person, time, place, and the task that is to be done.

Gary Christopher, a forty-year-old pastor in the inner city of San Diego reported in a conference in April 1995: "Eighteen months ago I owned a profitable beauty shop and a beauty aids business, and my wife was a public school teacher. The Lord told me to sell my business and to start a mission in San Diego. Last year the Lord led us to start a school, kindergarten through eighth grade, and the Lord has led us to open a home for unwed teenage mothers. We feed people every Sunday after worship. We now have more that 200 people each Sunday morning and the Lord has promised us that in another few years we will have 1,500 people worshiping each Sunday. The Lord has been good to us."

In the same meeting, which I was leading for church planters and potential church planters, Tony spoke of the Lord's call on his life to plant a church about three years ago in Elk Grove, California. Three years later the congregation averaged 335 in attendance. Mel and Rick spoke of the Lord's call on their lives to start a new church in Fremont in January 1995 and they had 234 in attendance the following Easter Sunday. They are examples of persons who stand to speak and say without hesitance, "This is what the Lord told me to do," and they usually indicate the geographic location he designated.

The Apostle Paul spoke of his personal call:

> After that, King Agrippa, I was not disobedient to the heavenly vision, but declared first to those in Damascus, then in ... Judea, and also to the Gentiles, that they should repent and turn to God and do deeds consistent with repentance.
>
> (Acts 26:19–20)

Moses reported how he experienced his call with considerable detail:

> God called him out of the bush, "Moses, Moses!" And he said, "Here I am." Then he said, "Come no closer! Remove the sandals from your feet, for the place on which you are standing is holy ground."
> (Exodus 3:4b–5)

I must refer to my personal story once again: It has been my experience that I have felt definitely impressed to take the ministerial assignment offered me each time I have made a pastoral move. Laura and I both felt led by the Lord when I was invited to Bellefontaine, Ohio, as youth and music minister. When we journeyed to Yazoo City fourteen months later to pastor a church in the Mississippi Delta, we again felt divinely directed. Three years later I was desperately wanting to return to seminary so that I would be a better equipped pastor and felt the Lord directing in that move. Sikeston, Missouri, was our sure call when I completed seminary. A three-month-old church in Columbus, Ohio, called us in 1965 and we had nearly a ten-year ministry with them.

Following that very satisfying experience, I resisted with some determination the call to work with a national agency of the Church of God—the Missionary Board. I was sure that the Missionary Board would not meet my minimal three criteria for employment. Reluctantly I agreed to an interview. All my objections were removed the first few minutes that Laura and I met with Executive-Secretary Lester Crose, Don Johnson, and Clair Shultz. Our call has been just as definite in our moves to Casper, Wyoming, where we pastored a fast-growing congregation for nine years, and to the Board of Church Extension of the Church of God where I now serve as Minister for Church Growth. We wept when we left each of these places and still shed tears as we think of the people and events that enriched our lives.

These experiences convinced me of a specific will of God for my life, for our lives—Laura and me. I am not saying that my assignments were all laid out when I was born at 1632 Clay Avenue in Charleston, West Virginia. It is more than likely that God said on that day, "What am I going to do with this fellow?"

Perhaps I am projecting what I have experienced as a norm for every other Christian. That is not my intent. From what I have read and observed, however, it appears to me that God has created us with unique personalities and has, as the scriptures say, given us a variety of gifts that qualify each of us for special ministries.

God's Will for a Congregation?

An additional aspect of this whole idea of the Lord's general and specific will is of interest to members of a church:

Does God have a general and specific will for each congregation of the church? Let us affirm what Barry Callen has stated in the title of the biography of pioneer Church of God preacher D. S. Warner—*It's God's Church!* Whatever our rhetoric, it is sad when we forget it is God's church when we are involved in congregational planning, congregational government, and congregational vision; especially when difficulties arise in the life and ministry of the church.

Yes, God has a general will for the church and you

Yes, God has a general will for his church and you can find that expressed in many places in the New Testament. Examples of these scriptures are as follows:

> All who believed were together and had all things in common, they would sell their possessions and goods and distribute the proceeds to all, as any had need. Day by day, as they spent much time together in the temple, they broke bread at home and ate their food with glad and generous hearts, praising God and having the goodwill of all the people. And day by day the Lord added to their number those who were being saved.
> (Acts 2:44–47)

> The gifts he gave were that some would be apostles, some prophets, some evangelists, some pastors and teachers, to equip the saints for the work of ministry, for building up the body of Christ, until all of us come to the unity of the faith and of the knowledge of the Son of God, to maturity, to the measure of the full stature of Christ.
> (Ephesians 4:11–13)

The Long-Range Planning Committee of the Leadership Council of the Church of God invited pastors and other leaders from all over the country to meet in January 1995 to express the vision of the church. What resulted was called a Vision-Action Statement. This is what these leaders said every Church of God congregation should do:

- Worship the Lord
- Reach the lost
- Disciple believers
- Equip for ministry
- Celebrate the unity of the body of believers
- Live out the love of Christ

It is an excellent summary of what every Church of God congregation must be doing if it dares to identify itself as God's church. In fact, any body of believers will be involved in those activities. It is a general call to all local congregations to be the complete, total witness of the body of Christ in the community.

A Congregation's Specific Call

Each congregation has a specific call to ministry, also. Two congregations in Kansas City are examples. Several years ago Gary Kendall led a group of Church of God people in planting a new congregation in Olathe. They met in a school building for nine years and then built a lovely structure for worship, education, and fellowship. In 1995 they averaged more than 350 in worship on Sunday morning. From the beginning they said it was their purpose to plant a new church out of their congregation every three years. Fred Bruner was brought on staff as associate pastor for a year and went to Lenexa with a group to plant a church that now is a growing, self-sustaining congregation with one hundred in attendance. Another church was started nearby with the encouragement of but not totally sponsored by, the Olathe congregation. Troy Redstone joined the staff of the Olathe congregation and began a new congregation based on a coffee house ministry.

Across town John Harvey pastors a multiethnic church of about 150 persons. The congregation is the foundation stone for an organization that rebuilds homes for people who cannot afford to buy homes in the usual way. In cooperation with Bank IV and City

Vision, a community organization he has created, John Harvey has helped a church discover and realize its unique ministry.

It is that unique ministry that gives a congregation vitality and energy. It is a realization that God has something special for us to do and we are going to do that ministry. This church has a special call under God. It is a wonderful opportunity for ministry in that community. It is both a strength and a challenge when congregations realize "the community needs our congregation's ministry and that ministry will not be done if we don't do it."

Each congregation repeatedly comes to those junctures where it can rediscover and realize anew its mission and ministry and enter into both with vitality. The church certainly wants to serve its members and constituents; each member needs to receive ministry and an opportunity to serve. The church's ministry cannot be decided on the basis of the needs of one group without concern for others, though the affluent and the educated need to hear the gospel as much as anyone.

The church's unique and special role in a community can only be comprehended and realized as it commits itself to be and do its unique ministry. The will of God is not discovered in a combination of opinions or a reduction of options to the lowest common denominator of ideas. The will of the Lord is done in the church only as we courageously set ourselves to discover that will and energetically enter into God's plan for us. I have some ideas of what that is for the congregation and community of which I am a part. You probably have some convictions about your church's ministry, too. It is important that we discover what God's ideas are before we become too enamored with our own.

God focuses on people like Moses, Paul, and John the Baptist with divine calls for specific roles. Many of us have a specific inspiration for vocation, in response to a similar call on our lives. Others may sense only a general call to accept salvation and live for the Lord. All of us are called into the fellowship of believers—the church—to live out the love of Christ in all of our communities—home, city, and world.

> Ponder and Process
>
> **Action Process**
> Counsel with your pastor or a respected leader of your congregation, seek his or her guidance, and then proceed with the ministry that you believe the Lord has been leading you to do. It will take courage and wisdom, but try it.
>
> **Meditation Process**
> Recall specific times in your life, if any, that you have sensed divine leadership. Was it a sudden and sure impression or a growing awareness?
>
> (continued)

Discussion Process

Read in unison Ephesians 4:11–13 (noting there may be different translations).

Divide the group into two teams. Ask one to affirm and defend this idea:

God expects us to love him and love people. We have the freedom to serve God and serve our fellow human beings in any place and in any way we choose.

Instruct the second team to affirm and defend this:

God has a specific assignment for us and will at times be adjusting the assignment and may change the place we are to serve.

Review the merits of each statement. Ask which statement is more true for persons in the group (they may have already done this in their "debate").

Read the Vision-Action Statement:
- Worship
- Reach the lost
- Disciple believers
- Equip for ministry
- Celebrate the unity of the body of believers
- Live out the love of Christ

Give examples of how your congregation is doing each of these.

Ask three persons to state what they believe to be the unique ministry of your congregation to the people of your community. Ask three other persons to evaluate how well your congregation is carrying out its unique ministry and how they might assist the effort.

Sing the chorus of *Have Thine Own Way, Lord,* or this hymn:

> A charge to keep I have,
> A God to glorify,
> A never-dying soul to save,
> And fit it for the sky.
> To serve the present age,
> My calling to fulfill,
> O may it all my pow'rs engage,
> To do my Master's will! Amen.
> —Charles Wesley

Chapter 6

THE TIME FACTOR

"Everyone has the same amount of time," and "Everyone has twenty-four hours a day, no more or no less," are clichés that sound all right but don't tell the whole story. Few of us have unlimited hours to give to the organization, programs, fellowships, and ministries of the congregation. What are some human limitations to the use of time in the life of the local church?

1. Limited Hours

Each person has a limited number of hours he or she can give to the local church, for any purpose. Reality is apparent when we take a quick glance at one person's daily schedule. Adele's schedule includes eight hours sleep; ten hours for working, getting ready for and traveling to and from work; two more hours for meal preparation and consumption with four hours left for all other necessary relational and living tasks. Saturdays and Sundays include shopping for food, clothing, and other essentials; occasional entertainment; time with her spouse; time with children; getting ready to start the week again with the house and clothes in good order; as well as time for worship and fellowship with the church family.

Adele's schedule does not have twenty-four available hours—most of them are obligated; family and personal interests are vying for the few discretionary hours. To be sure, a few persons in each congregation are able to control business and family obligations in such a way as to have more hours for discretionary use, and at least a few Christians tend to give a good portion of their time to the church. Even so, the schedule listed, and the one that follows are more typical. One is a working woman's schedule, but her husband has a similar one, and their schedules are not unusual. The time factor is a part of the human factor in the life of the local congregation.

Time has always been a precious commodity but some analysts are saying that whereas in previous generations members may have been more prone to give time than money to the local church, it is probably true that Christians have become just as restrictive in the amount of total time they will give to church interests.

Another factor is that many Christians do not consider time in church or in church activities as the best way to live out their Christian commitment; an increasing number of persons do not equate involvement in a local church as equivalent to Christian commitment. Our focus, however, is on the limited time most of us have for any activity, including worship and work with our local church. It has been suggested that active members can give only four to five hours per week, including the hours involved in worship services.

Kinsey's Schedule

I get up at seven o'clock and get on the school bus at 7:50 A.M. Classes begin at 8:25 A.M. and we are in classes until 11:05 when we go for lunch. We go back to classes from 11:35 A.M. to 2:30 P.M.; then I have basketball practice from 2:30 to about 4 P.M., or later if we have a game. I get home about 4:15 P.M. and go outside and play basketball or run. Our family has supper at about 5:30 P.M. and then I play basketball with dad or go over to the college gym or to the tennis club. At about 8 P.M. I do homework and maybe watch TV at the same time. Usually I take a shower at 8:30 and go to bed about 9.

Some evenings I play with my brother and sister—football, basketball, and races—and with dad; sometimes I go down the street to my friend Lauren's house. Saturday I might go shopping with mother, or go visit my grandparents in Warsaw. I also work on school projects on Saturday. Sundays I go to Sunday school and church. Mom cooks a roast on Sunday or we go out with our group—five families that celebrate birthdays together. Sunday is family night, but I look forward to being in youth fellowship next year.

—Kinsey Heberling, age 11

2. Limited Responsibilities

The number of responsibilities one person can handle effectively is limited. Many persons cannot give more than a few hours and many more choose not to give any significant time to the ministries of the local church, beyond participation in the Sunday morning worship service. In every congregation, though, a few persons give large blocks of time to the work of the church. They do so for a variety of reasons and each individual probably has more than one motive. Some may be generous with time because their business interests permit them a great deal of free time that they choose to use in the interest of the local church. Others are highly motivated persons who find personal fulfillment and a sense of call in church work and simply crowd extra time for the church into busy schedules. Still others are compulsive and have to be involved extensively and be obsessed with anything of which they are a part.

> **A New Currency**
>
> The new currency of life is not money but T-I-M-E. For this younger generation, free time has become more valuable than money. Thus, they do not tend to work overtime or take work home at night. With all the activities and pastimes available to them, Busters [born between 1965 and 1983] are busier than their Boomer parents [born 1946–1964] were at the same age.
>
> With the many demands on the Buster's time, structured church activities are often not top priorities. This means that Busters will probably be at fewer church activities than their Boomer parents. But Busters enjoy unstructured activities and will respond to those who are willing to spend time with them. The best way to touch their hearts for Christ is to simply spend time doing things with them.
>
> —Gary L. McIntosh (148)

Some retired persons may also give large blocks of time, but contrary to a false perception that persists, most retired persons are not bored persons waiting for someone to give them something to do. Retired persons often have family, travel, and avocation interests, and they, too, have limited hours available for church work. Another group: a few persons are hyperactive and find the church a wonderful outlet for their exceptional energy.

No one person can do everything best in the local church, and an unhealthy climate is generated when people try. Pastors are as guilty as laypersons in presuming "if you want it done right, do it yourself." It is the nature of a healthy church that no one has the gifts to do everything. (See the instructions about spiritual gifts in Romans 12, 1 Corinthians 12, and Ephesians 4.) Persons who accept multiple roles often think more highly of their indispensability than they should; well-intentioned, they are blind to the fact that their way of doing a task is not necessarily the best.

When a member of the church takes on too many responsibilities some negative results may occur. These negative results can become entrenched and be the accepted pattern for doing the work of the church for generations. A person giving major portions of time to a program or ministry of the congregation often comes to feel ownership of the program or ministry.

Ownership often means the person cannot separate his or her identity from the project itself; a criticism of the program is taken personally, for instance. (Remember, this is a human response. You and I are humans and this ownership malady can upset any of us.)

Martyrdom is another pitfall for persons who get overly involved. Many necessary ministries of the local church demand extensive time commitments on the part of pastors and laypersons; however, again we are talking about one person being involved extensively, often to the exclusion of others. A man may feel that he is the only one who is really concerned about his ministry and if he doesn't do it, no one else is sufficiently committed to do it. A woman may feel that she has to work hard in order to guarantee the success of a program and come to feel a bit sorry for herself that she has to spend so many hours while others are in personal activities that are more fun. A sense of suffering, with the feeling that no one is caring about the ministry, is probably a reliable indicator that a person is overly involved.

A sense of being indispensable also sneaks into the mind of a member who has too many responsibilities in the church. A companion of this feeling is a desire for control. When persons feel indispensable they often feel they must control the program, aggressively resist any efforts to modify it, and if they lose control some less thoughtful and gifted person will destroy the program. Think of the stress (distress) in one's life that is generated when a person feels indispensable and thus must control the whole environment of a church program or ministry!

The people factor has several dimensions:

- First, no one person is able to take care of a number of responsibilities well in the local church without distorting the church.
- Second, human beings tend to "take over" when they give exceptional time to an effort, and when one person takes over a church ministry as his or her own, others are excluded.
- Third, it is difficult for persons who are carrying many responsibilities in the church and exerting personal control of programs and events to realize what they are doing—their perspective becomes distorted.

- Fourth, even persons who give significant blocks of time to church work have limitations, and when they go beyond those limitations personal health and relationships suffer.

Every person has a limited amount of time he or she can give to the services and ministries of the local church.

3. Church Organization and the Volunteer's Time

The organizational structure of the local church can dictate a misuse of the time members give for the work of the local church. Too many pastors and lay leaders resort to the approach of the farmer who was plowing his field. The traveler observed a single mule, wearing blinders, hitched to a plow. The farmer yelled, "Giddyup, Pete! Giddyup, Herb! Giddyup, Bill! Giddyup, Jeb!"

The traveler was puzzled and after some time asked the farmer, "Say mister, how many names does that mule have?"

The farmer said, "Just one. His name is Peter."

"Then why do you call out all those names?"

"Well," said the farmer, "If Ol' Pete knew he was doing all this work alone, I couldn't make him do it. But if he thinks he's got three other mules working alongside of him, he does the whole job by himself."

Pastors and lay leaders have been known to use deceptive methods to get persons to accept church assignments.

Pastor Kent Adcock has just left my office. In passing, he said something to this effect: "Our church is focusing on outreach. We are interested and active in meeting the needs of people outside our church. It has been a change; just a year or so ago we were more concerned about how a program would benefit us. What made the change possible is having a single leadership group of five persons. They give direction to the work of the church and create task forces for specific assignments. Once the job is completed, the task force disbands. This enables people to do ministry, also. If they see something they can do to help someone, they no longer have to go through several committees "that have an interest" but can enlist other persons and meet needs. We like it better this way and are enjoying it more." Pastor Milton Grannum of the fast-growing and community-oriented congregation in Philadelphia echoes Kent's thoughts. He encourages a simple organization that frees the members of the congregation to do ministry.

One way the church organizational structure may waste volunteer time is with interlocking committees and boards. For instance, in one church I pastored a person who was asked to coordinate the athletic teams of the church discovered that he was also responsible to attend the meetings of the Board of Christian Education and the Church Council—a total of at least four hours of responsibility each month for which he felt he was not prepared; he was not even interested. A person elected to chair the trustees may be surprised to find she must also attend meetings of the council. In addition, the council may be the building committee and also the pastoral search committee. That which was thought to be a manageable commitment of a few hours a month can become a group of meetings involving several hours each week for several months.

The interlocking memberships contribute to another factor that has a devastating effect on ministry: persons spend all of their available time in meetings! This is tragic, for many of the highly motivated persons who will serve on boards and committees are also persons who could be involved more effectively in evangelism, education, and other servant and leadership ministries. The guidance of the organization is an essential ministry but too often it becomes the primary ministry, and that is a wasteful and too common distortion of the church.

Adele, whose daily schedule we outlined, has excellent relational gifts and is a deeply committed Christian who loves her church. She probably can give about two hours per week beyond time reserved for Sunday worship and participation in a small prayer group. She is popular and is asked to serve on a standing committee, becomes the chair, and thus must also meet with the Church Council. Recently she was asked to participate in a training session for personal evangelists. She acknowledged great interest but had to decline because of the time she had committed to the committee and the council.

The organizational structure of the local church may be robbing the church of some of its most effective evangelists, teachers, and servants. We need not blame the devil for working against the church when, in fact, we have persons so involved in filling slots in a complicated organization that it essentially immobilizes many of our most capable lay ministers!

What are some ways we can assure better use of volunteer time in the local church? We will mention a few.

Focus on Ministry

Intentionally structure the church so that the focus is on ministries instead of on the organization. It is not easily done, for one thing, because so many churches have viewed the organizational structure as essential and as the acceptable way of doing church. One pastor has said, "How can we get anything done if we don't have these committees and boards?" He was not aware that the reason for the meeting was that the church he pastored was not getting the work of the kingdom done. He is like many of us who cannot see any different way of structuring than the way we have been structured.

Those with congregational government may find the road to simpler organization a viable option more readily than those churches whose organizations are indicated by a book of discipline or by a national church judicatory. Ways can be found to simplify.

The church can enlist persons for what they have determined are essential ministries. Simple organization can then be created to enable the ministries. One result can be this: the church does evangelism and gifted persons are enlisted for that task; the care of the building is entrusted to persons who are not particularly gifted in personal relationships. See the difference: The primary use of available volunteer time is for ministries rather than routine and traditional tasks such as keeping the building and annual programs going. All tasks are important, but in the life of the church too often traditional tasks take the time and money and ministries are left without adequate personnel and finance.

Recognize Gifts and Interests

Pastors and lay leaders can give careful attention to recognizing persons' gifts and where they can best serve. Many congregations have a spiritual gifts workshop for members using a manual and workbook called *Discover Your Gifts.* An aid a congregation can prepare is an attractive brochure listing all the areas of ministry in the local church, including coaching athletic teams, teaching classes, ushering, visiting, and singing in the choir. Another way to do this is to circulate twice a year a form listing ministries in which members may enlist.

Having served as a pastor and as a consultant for churches, I know that too often persons are enlisted to fill vacancies, such as taking the place of a junior high class teacher who recently moved or serving as a representative of a particular group, say as a new person on the council. Both the "filling a vacancy" and the "representative new person" methods short circuit the whole concept of spiritual giftedness and divine call, which we believe is a part of every person's ministry. Persons are of most value to the church when they are helped to discover a place of service for which they sense some divine equipment and call.

Pastors and lay leaders are the key persons in making sure members find these spiritually fulfilling roles. It is the best way to use the few precious hours persons have available for work in the local church.

The best organizational structure is simple and provides for a variety of ways to carry out ministries. In some church traditions, bylaws of local congregations were intended to meet legal requirements for holding property and dispensing finances. Over a period of time bylaws started indicating the organization for and the implementation of ministries—everything had to be in the bylaws. This change tended to limit ministries: for instance, only the board of Christian education could initiate a training class.

The national organization of the WOMEN OF THE CHURCH OF GOD has made great strides in recent years in simplifying their organizational structure. Not too long ago every local unit had a list of offices for which it attempted to provide a person, however small the local group. The result often created an organizational structure more impressive than the size of the group. The national organization now encourages a simplified approach to leadership. Where formerly they offered one model for the local women's organization, they now encourage women to discover different models for women's meetings and women's fellowships. The local groups continue to give a major emphasis to missions but have expanded to a ministry for the whole person in a variety of models.

Train by Mentoring

Mentoring is a foundation for wise use of volunteer time. In mentoring, a person who is experienced in a ministry gives time and creates a relationship with another person who seeks to learn how to do the ministry. It is coaching at its best. Teachers best teach teachers in the classroom. Ushers best teach ushers by working closely and patiently with new volunteers. Evangelism is best understood when one who is experienced takes another with him who wants to learn.

Other methods have long been used in the church. Persons have, at times, been given responsibilities without instruction and little opportunity to gain experience. Others have been handed a book and a written job description and were surprised that neither seemed to include information relevant to the real task. For years progressive groups have provided training conferences for ministry; the African-American congregations of the Church of God have trained members for ministry with summer conferences covering a broad spectrum of subjects and conventions focusing on special ministries such as ushering.

All of these training methods are of value, but mentoring, the along-side-of relationship, is the best way to prepare persons for effective ministry in the local church.

Mentoring enables a person to learn and practice in a rhythm that results in growth. Mentoring takes a long time, compared with other methods, but the result is that the person is equipped to do the task well.

Board Meetings Can Be Improved
Transform board and committee meetings. Not many persons really enjoy committee meetings and many look forward to serving out their term. Committee and board meetings are often a bore, deal with minutiae, and dampen enthusiasm. People are likely to leave a committee or board meeting pleased, more than anything else, that the meeting is over. It doesn't have to be so. If members have only a few hours to be with each other each week or month, then each one of these people probably needs some inspiration and assurance. Why couldn't we change our meetings so that they meet those needs?

> **Functions of the Mentor**
> The mentor has several continuing and overlapping functions during the whole process of training. Relating to and teaching the mentoree includes
> **Enrichment**: providing treasures for the learner that will be a lasting resource for his or her ministry. The treasures include
> • the gift of oneself in friendship
> • information on how best to do the task(s)
> • experience together in doing ministry.
> **Encouragement**: assuring the learner of personal support by
> • freely giving compliments on tasks done well and
> • generously expressing concern, verbally and nonverbally, for the person, especially when the learner is discouraged.
> **Evaluation**: assisting the learner in assessing progress by caring enough
> • to be kind in evaluations and
> • honest about successes and failures.
> **Enabling**: conveying strength for the task by
> • directing the learner to resources and
> • giving permission for the learner to venture into ministry.

Charles M. Olsen says we can and has written a book, *Transforming Church Boards*. The idea he sets forth:

> The individual board member is no longer seen as a political representative but as a spiritual leader. The board or council is no longer seen as a group of corporate managers, but as the people of God in community. The meeting is no longer seen as a litany of reports and decisions held together by "book-end" prayers but as "worshipful work."
>
> (xii–xiii)

Olsen explains:

> The collective board is not to see itself as a coordinating cabinet or an advisory group but as the people of God in community. The group is the body of Christ, with members having varying gifts, wisdom, and functions. As such the group's life is formed by scripture, prayer, silent waiting, witnessing, and serving (10).

Committee reports are replaced with a four-practice model that includes in every meeting story telling and history giving, biblical and theological reflection, prayerful discernment, and visioning the future. The single-page agenda is one determined by consent and items are ranked in order of importance so that the group will give its energies to the more significant issues.

Church groups that have attempted to transform their boards into worshipful communities have discovered inspired and rejoicing groups emerging from their sessions.

It can be done. Inspired and informed people volunteer when they are refreshed and uplifted. Who wants to attend board and committee meetings that are routine or business-as-usual? Time given to board and committee meetings can become meaningful and rewarding and the transformation will undoubtedly spill over into the total fellowship of the church.

People will rejoice and be refreshed when participating on boards and committees that become worshipful communities.

Ponder and Process

Action Process

Choose a person whose responsibilities are different from yours. Observe the person and ask about his or her schedule. List obligations the person has of which you were not aware.

Meditation Process

A very few hours or minutes are available to use as you please. What is one experience to which you can give discretionary time that will enrich your life?

Discussion Process

Select two persons (before the time of the meeting) to read Psalm 90:1–12 responsively, alternating verses. Select another to read Ephesians 5:15–16.

Provide a sheet of paper and a writing surface for each person. Ask each to write out a schedule for a typical day; take a brief time for comments.

Encourage each person to indicate on a piece of paper the number of hours he or she has available for the worship services and ministry in the church. Ask several persons to explain their answers.

Ask if there are persons in the group who feel they have overobligated themselves to church activities.

Ask the group to help list on the *left* side of a sheet of paper or chalkboard the responsibilities in the church that are primarily for the purpose of keeping the organization going—building maintenance, and the like.

On the *right* side of the paper or chalkboard list those tasks that are primarily a ministry directed to persons. Ask if any would like to be trained for a specific ministry. If one or two persons say yes, ask them to identify the ministry in which they have an interest.

Request that two or three persons lead in prayer, but encourage them not to be threatened by moments of silence. Pray together the Mizpah:

> The LORD watch between you and me,
> when we are absent one from the other.
> —Genesis 31:49

Chapter 7

THE PASTOR PERSON

Laura and I were traveling to Indiana early in 1988 to meet with seminary students and pastors from central Indiana to discuss burnout. As we boarded the plane at Denver's Stapleton Airport, we were surprised and delighted to see our friends Gerald and Lorena Marvel. Jerry and Rena were invited to co-lead the sessions at the Anderson University School of Theology. Eventually Jerry and I were seated together and Lorena with Laura. Jerry said something like, "Oral, I guess they want us to tell them how to do it, this burnout stuff." Jerry began the statement with his typical impish smile but then was serious when he said, "It was the scariest thing I have ever gone through." I wanted to hear the story and asked him to continue.

Jerry's Story

Jerry had been hospitalized for a few weeks several months previous to our meeting on the plane. He had taken four or five weeks for recovery in a Kentucky retreat home owned by a friend. Jerry wrote his story for our national church paper later:

> For the past few years I had been pastoring a church and trying to take care of speaking engagements across the country. Each week I prayed, "God, just get me through this week and next week will be better ... just get me through the services today, and next Sunday will be better."
> The summer wore on and my state worsened: the doctor called it emotional, biological depression. We [Rena and I] had prayer; later, she asked me, "How is it going?"
> "God answered prayer," I said, "I'm over this. I'm on my way." I had two good days.
> Later that week I was sinking even deeper. But I was ashamed to come back and tell Rena. I tried to hide it. I got so desperate I called my daughter in Indianapolis; I didn't want to admit to myself or anyone else that I couldn't lick this problem. I didn't even want anyone to know I had a problem.
> On September 2, I came home in the afternoon, sat down on the couch, and started to cry. I cried and I cried and I cried—uncontrollably.

Jerry told his wife he was going for a walk but Rena persuaded him to go to a medical doctor who is a member of their church. The doctor admitted him to the hospital and Jerry found himself, "way up on the ninth floor, on the Walanta River side that night, crying and staring out the window." For the first time since he was a teenager he was not in control of his life—people told him when to eat, when to sleep, and to stay in his bed at night.

Later, after a month in Kentucky, he returned "to one of the most fearful times I've ever experienced." He was again to preach to his congregation. Jerry explains,

"God said, 'Gerald, just tell them what happened to you and where you've been and that you need help to keep going' " (story taken from VITAL CHRISTIANITY, July 24, 1988, 2–3).

What Happened to You, Oral?

Jerry asked me about my experience and I attempted to tell about it briefly. Though it is not easy to talk about, when I get started it is difficult to stop. In October I had come home at noon from my study at the church. Collapsing on a kitchen chair, I announced, "Laura, I am quitting." Laura immediately responded, "If you really feel your ministry is over in Casper, I want you to quit. But, if you are quitting just because you're worn out and sick, I think we should do something else."

My physician, Dr. Tom Burke, had been trying to help me overcome a "flu bug" and other repeated infections. Laura asked if she could call Dr. Burke.

I was surprised to hear my self answering, "You can call him if you want. It won't make any difference. He hasn't been able to help me." It was not my practice to let anyone talk to my doctor about my health; I reserved that responsibility for myself.

Laura telephoned the doctor and told him she was concerned about my repeated illnesses that seemed never totally to go away. She listened for a long time and later she told me what he said: "If Oral were my Catholic priest, we would send him to a retreat center in New Mexico for a year of rest and recovery. His problem basically is not physical; he is emotionally exhausted."

Next she asked (or maybe declared), "Do you mind if I call Norman?" Norman was chair of our Church Council. It was a strange feeling. I had abandoned all my resistance to anyone taking charge of my life and was open to whatever she wanted to do.

A telephone call to Norman resulted in the convening of the Church Council the next evening. Following their meeting, Norm told me they had voted for me to take a six-month sabbatical with full pay and insisted I was not to worry about anything.

With reluctance I agreed to their offer and began a sabbatical a few weeks later. On a recovery trip to the Midwest and in an educational experience at Fuller Seminary I began to know what physical and emotional health felt like again. I can recall to this day my feeling of euphoria when a "flu" that had stayed with me for weeks was finally totally healed. It was on a sunny morning traveling south in Illinois. It was marvelous. Incidentally, I took only three months leave. The associate pastor of my congregation was an excellent preacher and I didn't want the people to become too accustomed to his preaching!

Sometimes, experiences from childhood affect our self-esteem. As a result, we work extra hours to gain approval, and compliments on our sermons and ministry are very important to us—more important than they should be. Many persons in the ministry—many persons in all walks of life—have discovered a security in the church that was not present in their home and that accounts for some of their deep commitment to the church. Even so, some of us bring somewhat dysfunctional personality patterns into our vocation—we keep trying to earn love, approval, and warm praise while we talk about grace and acceptance for others. If only totally normal persons were permitted in church-related vocations, especially the pastoral ministry, we would be woefully short of leaders.

David, Too?

It is not only those ministers who have had unhealthy childhood experiences that are crushed by the pastoral ministry. David Shultz's office was next to mine when we both worked for the Missionary Board of our church. David is an exceptionally gifted speaker, with a resonant voice and good looks—a person who is both disciplined and artistic. Quite frankly, I thought David had everything anyone could want. He even misted the plants in my office, and I didn't even know that "plants like to be misted."

David became the pastor of a church that had stalled in its growth. He led the congregation in the process of leasing their building to a local industry and moving into a high school auditorium. Following the construction of a new facility, the congregation experienced rapid growth and expansion of its ministries.

Then something happened. David began to slip into depression. Over two years his condition worsened until he could barely prepare a sermon. His wife said he became a joyless individual who was very unlike the man she had married. Finally, he requested a leave of absence from his congregation, which was granted on condition that he receive professional counseling. David gratefully agreed.

Over the next three months he began a healing process, which he says is continuing, years later. Some of the elements feeding his depression were a classic midlife crisis, repressed and unresolved anger toward the church, and unresolved issues from his childhood on the mission field. David had left home at the age of thirteen to live with a pastor's family while David's parents continued in missionary service abroad.

In his forties, with the cumulative stress of leading a fast-growing church, David had to stop to review and reestablish his life. It was tough on him and all those who love him. David continues to be one of those persons whom I greatly respect because of his personality and gifts, but now even more so because he is more aware of his humanness.

David has written insightfully of his experience:

> At the heart of my problem was a flawed understanding of God. Although I had been raised in the church, I somehow wrongly concluded that God loves some people more than others: I thought he loved Christians more than non Christians, and among Christians he loved missionaries most, pastors second, and the rest third. In other words, we have to earn his favor. I thought I had to earn answers to prayer with sacrifice or fasting. I thought that weakness and failure were signs that God had abandoned me.
>
> This breakdown, although painful, was the means God used to teach me what he is really like. I learned that God treasures us, not for what we do, but for who we are. I learned that I am not responsible for what other Christians do or don't do.

I learned I am fallible, and it's okay to be human. My body will cave in if I don't take care of it. Even though I am spiritually victorious, my emotions are not immune to breakdown. Besides this, it's okay for other people to be human, too.

If you conclude that this is an experience of a few overzealous and self-centered pastors, then you will make a mistake. These experiences are not rare; they are common. The sad truth is that many pastors go through the depth of defeat, discouragement, and depression and no one notices except to suggest that it may be time for the pastor to consider another assignment.

The Pastor Is a Human Being

The greatest mistake that pastors make about themselves is this one: they forget they are human. The biggest mistake that churches make about their pastors is this one: they forget that their pastors are human. The Docetists were a heretical group in the early church who said that Christ only appeared to be in human form; really he was totally spiritual; a similar heresy is to deny the humanness of pastors.

Pastors and churches do well to remember the humanness of the pastor from at least three perspectives:

1. Vocational Perspective

The pastor and the church meet at the point of vocation. Church members have enlisted this person to be their pastor because of the pastor's divine call, ministerial training, and experience. This is the pastor's work, what he or she does to fulfill the call and, as is true with others, to earn a living. The pastor and the congregation, therefore, create an accountability structure to help the pastor understand what tasks are to be done and what relationships are be to developed. The pastor is a human being and needs to understand what other human beings are expecting.

> **A Pastor Is Expected to**
> - Live an exemplary life;
> - Be available at all times to all people for all purposes;
> - Lead the church to grow numerically;
> - Balance wisdom with leadership and love;
> - Teach people the deeper truths of the faith in ways that are readily approachable in all life situations;
> - Be a committed family man who demonstrates what it means to be the spiritual head of the family, a lover of one woman, and a positive role model for children;
> - Keep pace with the latest trends and developments in church life;
> - Build significant relationships with members of the congregation;
> - Represent the church in the community;
> - Grow spiritually;
> - Run the church in a crisp, professional, businesslike manner without taking on a cold, calculating air.
> - In the typical business, the standards for evaluation are spelled out in advance. In most of the churches we have studied, there are only vague criteria for assessment, and the application of those criteria tends to be rather loose.
>
> —George Barna (1993, 52, 145–146)

Pastors and churches often forget the pastoral ministry is a job. Oh, it is much more for it directly relates to the eternal concerns of people. Nonetheless, it is a job and it is, therefore, not the total experience of life. No vocation and no work should take all of the best hours of a person's week, even if that person is a pastor.

Some weeks ago I discovered that my secretary was taking home some work to do that she did not have time to do in the office. It is a joy to work with persons who are dedicated to their assignment and will put forth special efforts. Even so, I told her that we did not expect her to take work home; we had no right to her off-duty time, time that rightfully belonged to other interests of her life. Most pastors, as human beings, need that type of reminder.

Some pastors have to be helped to understand their workload and how to put in a "full day's work." Thoughtful lay leaders assist pastors who have not learned to do this. For the most part, though, pastors need a reminder that other areas of their lives demand time and that their pastoral work will have to wait when the tasks begin to encroach on the time necessary for healthy living. Too often lay persons praise pastors for working long hours, being away from home several nights a week, not taking a vacation, and always being on call. It is wrong to praise a pastor for that type of workaholism, and it eventually leads to personal collapse and a distorted sense of ministry—sometimes to the destruction of family life.

Pastors need accountability structures (not bosses) to guide them in making decisions about work and to make sure they don't work when they should be doing something else.

2. Personal Perspective

Pastors have personal needs for recreation, relaxation, and relationships—especially family relationships. The Meadow Park Church in Columbus, Ohio, had been in existence three months when they called me as pastor. We moved three hundred miles with four children, the youngest six weeks old, to begin our leadership of a congregation that met in a school—an uncommon place in those days, but it is where we met for nearly five years. After growth, a major construction program, and sacrificial living that few persons knew about, our family was in need of a vacation but we didn't know how we could arrange one.

> **Clergy Family Different?**
> For clergy, more than any other professionals, work and family systems plug all too easily into one another and significant changes in either system may be quicker to unbalance the other. Yet even that difference does not really make the clergy family "different." Rather, it means that in order to insure its overall family health, differentiation of self is more imperative.
> —Edwin H. Freedman (279)

Thank the Lord for Dr. Jack Hutchinson who spoke up one Monday evening during a meeting of the board of trustees, "I think that we should fire any pastor who won't take a vacation." There was only one pastor on the staff so his words were pretty directed. In a few weeks our family was on the road to Disney Land. A family in the church put the entrance tickets in our pockets just before we left and packed some snacks for the kids to open each day. We needed that! We needed persons who would push us to do what any healthy family should do. We needed some friends who would make sure we had the finances to have a good time when we arrived; we were consistently broke in those years. We needed some people to care about us—and our children—to help us with our personal perspective.

3. Spiritual Perspective

Isn't it amazing that what pastors and churches often forget about pastors is that they need time to nurture spirituality. Many pastors are so busy attending board and committee meetings, visiting persons who should be out calling on people themselves, and running business errands, that the pastor does not have time to be a growing spiritual person. It happens. It has happened to me and it happens to too many pastors.

Pastors have to have time to be alone to grow spiritually. Pastors need time to study, to think. The spiritual life of a pastor is enhanced as he or she finds time to seek counsel with a respected friend, to have a confessor. Pastors have to have time, place, and energy for personal renewal. When pastors and congregations do not understand the very human need of a pastor to develop spirituality, the result is a person guiding others in a quest for the Spirit, having himself or herself become a stranger to the Spirit.

Super-Human Assignment

Pastors are human beings, very natural creations of God, called to a supernatural task. The best scriptural summary of the pastoral vocation is given in Ephesians 4:11–13.

In this century Bible scholars have changed the punctuation marks in the English translation and the change helps us understand it is the responsibility of pastors and teachers to equip believers for ministries. We had too long thought this scripture was saying that pastors should "do the ministry." Often in church history it has been presumed that the clergy did ministry, and members of the church were ministered to and informed the pastor where he should be ministering. It was a generally accepted model when I entered the ministry, fresh out of college, in the 1950s.

> **Ephesians 4:11–13**
> The gifts he gave were that some would be apostles, some prophets, some evangelists, some pastors and teachers, to equip the saints for the work of ministry, for building up the body of Christ, until all of us come to the unity of the faith and of knowledge of the Son of God, to maturity, to the measure of the full stature of Christ.

Pastors and teachers were likely to possess a separate set of gifts in the mind of Paul, but his letters to the early church indicate the pastoring and teaching roles overlapped considerably. He instructed Timothy about leadership, evangelism, and teaching, among other things (1 Timothy 1:3; 3:14; 4:6; 2 Timothy 2:14–15; 4:5). Whatever, the roles came to be combined functionally in one person—pastor and teacher. Actually, the role of the pastor has come to include the responsibilities of all the leadership gifts mentioned in this scripture. The pastor is, more often than not, expected to be

- A priest to care for the believers (pastor literally means "shepherd");

- A prophet who proclaims the Word of the Lord;
- A teacher who instructs in the doctrine and practice of the faith;
- An evangelist who is responsible to persuade persons to follow Christ;
- An apostle, at least in some instances, as I have found, when spiritual leadership is expected for more than just the local church.

It is not unusual for one person to be expected to assume all of these leadership roles as a pastor. It is best to understand the pastoral assignment as that of a leader caring for the flock and instructing in the faith. It is a superhuman task! Whatever ways the scripture may be interpreted, the assignment is demanding.

According to Ephesians 4:11–13, the pastor has the following responsibilities:

A. Equip. The pastor is to equip believers for their ministries. The King James Version speaks of the perfection of the saints. The pastor is to help Christians round out and complete their understanding of the faith so they can serve people well.

B. Edify. The pastor is to edify the church and challenge those whom he is training to edify the church—that is, as some translations have it, "build up the church."

C. Lead Believers to Christian Maturity. The pastor has the responsibility to make persons knowledgeable of Christ and his teachings, but even more so the Spirit of Christ, the mind of Christ, the passion of Christ—to lead to full maturity.

The responsibility list for the pastors of many of our congregations includes additional functions such as

- extended visits and conversations with members,

- administration of the organization, and,
- yes, mowing the lawn and making sure the door is unlocked and locked before and after worship services.

Now, to be sure, none of those mundane responsibilities ever hurt anyone, but the role of the pastor is best defined when biblical responsibilities are placed first and given priority: equip, edify, lead to maturity. A pastor in some situations may be forgiven for talking to himself like a man in the supermarket who was pushing his grocery cart containing a screaming, yelling two-year-old. The fellow repeated phrases such as "Don't get excited, Albert," "Don't scream, Albert," "Don't yell, Albert."

A woman nearby said, "You certainly are to be commended for trying to soothe your son Albert."

The man responded soberly, "Lady, I'm Albert."

Humans Do the Superhuman

It is a wonder that it ever works. Can anyone pastor? Look around and you will find persons with long legs and short, with beards or clean-shaven faces, with skirts or trousers, handsome and not so handsome, intelligent and not so intelligent, talkative and quiet, who are pastoring and doing it very well. How in the world, especially in this world we live in, can that happen?

Prayer

A person who pastors well has to have the prayer of the church, especially of a few persons who have the gift of intercessory prayer.

It is with great warmth that I recall Friday mornings in my last pastorate. Fifteen to twenty-five men would meet at 6:30 A.M. to pray for the church, the unsaved, and especially Sunday's worship service. Sometimes we had coffee and rolls, but before we went our separate ways we left the fellowship/gymnasium area and went into the sanctuary. The pastor and associate pastors were asked to sit on the altar and the men would gather round them touching each pastor on the head, shoulder, or arm and pray for them as persons and for their ministry. Strength came through those arms into my body and soul, the Spirit of God flowing through the arms of members of the congregation who were identifying with their pastors. Enabling power came in those Friday morning experiences.

> **Ministers' Roles**
>
> In a major study done in 1934, the minister was seen to have five roles: teacher, preacher, worship leader, pastor, and administrator. A study done in 1980 found that these roles had almost doubled to nine [adding]: expected to have an open and affirming style, know how to foster friendship in the church, be aware of things denominational, and be able to lead the church's participation in political discussions as well as provide a witness against the world's injustices.
>
> By 1986 ... fourteen roles [in order] ... planning ability ... leading worship, sensitivity to the congregation ... spiritual development of the congregation, pastoral counseling of the needy, visiting the sick ... support the stewardship program ... administrative leadership ... involve the laity ... support the church's mission. And holding issues of social justice before the congregation was now last as a pastoral priority.
> —David F. Wells in Guiness (1992, 183)

Biblical Assignments

A person who pastors well will have biblical assignments. The pastor is called to lead, preach, and teach (as outlined earlier). There are other tasks and responsibilities but these are primary assignments that require many work hours and diligence. Extended conversations with members of the church, attendance to an array of committee and board meetings, and publishing a weekly news sheet are all tasks that are important but can consume all the pastor's time, thus leaving little time for the tasks for which he or she alone is uniquely gifted and called.

Many of the tasks that often dominate the time of a pastor can be delegated to other persons. No superhuman endowments are needed for the routine tasks in the church and pastors who are given these and similar tasks by their congregations will be disappointed because routine rather than fantastic experiences are the result. Pastors need divine appointments, tasks that can only be accomplished as they are enabled by God—leading, preaching, teaching. Pastors who give first attention to the biblical assignment will enable a church to grow and to minister.

Covenant

A person who pastors well will have a covenant with the congregation. The covenant may and probably should include a written understanding, a contract. More so, the congregation when calling a pastor will assure the pastor of financial support, positive participation in the life of the church, and positive response to his or her leadership. No church should offer less.

> **Nature of Covenant**
> Covenant implies that relationship is more important than performance, that belonging is more important than succeeding, that being is more important than doing. Contracts are conditional; covenants are essentially unconditional. But continuing "for better, for worse" is not embracing a self-inflicted death sentence or locking oneself in a relational prison. It is an invitation to go deeper with God and God's people. Without saying so most people want contracts—negotiated exchanges of goods and services—that can be broken if one partner breaks the contract. Churches easily fall into the trap of thinking they can define the pastoral ministry contractually, as an exchange of services in return for remuneration. But Christian ministry is essentially covenantal. There is a "for better, for worse" about it, a bonding and binding agreement to work this thing out for God's glory and for the upbuilding of the body of Christ because we belong together.
> —R. Paul Stevens and Phil Collins (3)

Growth

A person who pastors well will have opportunity for growth. To do the superhuman task of pastoring, a person has to keep growing. Methods of another generation have to be unlearned and new methods learned. Enthusiasms that endeared a young minister to a congregation will have to mature into wisdom as the congregation faces difficult challenges. A pastor has to have the encouragement and financial assistance to grow as a person; training is essential and is one of the wisest investments of the local church.

Appreciation

A person who pastors well has to hear expressions of appreciation. In another context, it would be well to talk to pastors about how to express appreciation to persons and encourage them as persons and believers. Thousands of congregations can choose to change their pattern and learn to express appreciation. It is a part of the whole arena of healthy relationships.

Compliments to pastors are in order. Some persons, for reasons beyond my comprehension, have decided that to compliment a pastor about his sermon, for instance, is feeding the ego (and some think that feeding the ego is bad). The pastor who has preached after having prepared for several hours is refreshed by kind complimentary words. Expressions that I have had spoken to me and heard spoken to other pastors include these:

"You spoke so meaningfully to me, pastor."

"Thanks for what you said this morning. It helped!"

"I needed a laugh more than anything today, pastor. I appreciate your humor."

"You will never know how much your call on my aunt this week meant to all of us."

"Tell that story at my funeral, and tell them they have to laugh."

"I just wanted to clap my hands when you urged us to go on."

A pastor can do superhuman things with a church when flooded with appreciative comments and notes. The pastor has to have appreciation and it lights a fire when a pastor hears those kind words. Even as I write I become emotional as I remember the congregations that

I have pastored and how many encouraged me every week for years; I remember a few persons who discovered something kind to say to me even when the quality of my work was not deserving of notice. Of course, in every church there were and are those who have negative comments. It comes with the territory. But those who convey a "thank you" or a compliment help propel a pastor to a superhuman ministry.

Ponder and Process

Action Process

Write a note of appreciation to the pastor or a member of the pastor's family.

Meditation Process

Provide two answers to the questions: Why is it important for the pastor to accept his or her humanness? Why does God call some persons to the pastoral ministry?

Discussion Process

First read and then lead the group in praying:

Let the words of our mouths and the meditations of our hearts be acceptable to you, O Lord, our rock and our redeemer (Psalm 19:14, adapted).

Review one of the pastor's stories provided in the first part of this chapter. Comments?

Pastoring a congregation of people is not like any other vocation. List ways it is different.

Identify two provisions a congregation may make for a pastor's family that will express special appreciation for their service.

List ways a congregation may become aware that their pastor is exhausted and needs an extended time for study and relaxation.

Would your congregation be enriched if everyone would become more generous with compliments? Identify three compliments members of your group will give your pastor this week.

Ask for prayer requests for the pastor(s) and enlist one or two persons to focus the group's prayer on the pastor(s) today.

Chapter 8

WHEN THE FUR FLIES

The engaged couple were young, both about eighteen. I was doing the premarital counseling and personality test, and as we discussed the potential hazards for newlyweds, I posed the question: "How do you handle disagreements?" The young bride-to-be assured me that they had never had a disagreement; they were "getting along perfectly."

The next question was obvious: "When you do have disagreements, what are some ways that you might handle them?"

She again responded, and her mate nodded in agreement, "We are so in love and so alike that we talk things through and don't disagree, and I don't see us ever seriously disagreeing."

The couple was not unusual in its idealism but a bit more naive than most. Many couples are equally convinced that they can easily handle anything that happens, with little difficulty.

The responses of the young bride and groom remind me of a woman lay leader in a congregation who said, "If we will just pray and talk we will not have any disagreements in our church." She was a mature Christian but very unaware of the realities of life, even life in the fellowship of the church. She thought, as many do, that difficulties between people do not arise in healthy churches. It is not so, "nor was it ever thus." Disagreements, arguments, misunderstandings, and sometimes conflicts happen in the best of churches. The truth is that members may spend significant time in prayer, but their prayers may be that the persons with whom they disagree will see the light and accept the truth in the matter. Persons who fail to see that differences, strong differences, do arise in the fellowship of the church are as naive as the young bride who could not foresee that she and her husband would ever seriously disagree. Lest it be stated too strongly: conflict is not desirable in the life of a church but it is inevitable.

A Storm's Coming

Casper Mountain is just south of the city of Casper, Wyoming. The city's elevation is about five thousand feet and the mountain about eight thousand feet. Halfway up the mountain is an overlook where you can see for seventy or eighty miles on a clear day. Laura and I stood there one day and observed a dark cloud moving in from the west. We knew a storm was on the way. We canceled some plans for a leisurely day on top of the mountain and returned to our home. We saw a storm coming and prepared for it.

Another story: two years ago Laura was turning left at an intersection second in line behind another automobile. The light changed to red for oncoming traffic; the car in front of her turned and she followed. An oncoming truck failed to stop and hit her automobile broadside, destroying it. Though she suffered some injuries, she has now recovered from most of her pain and drives rather freely again.

> ### Close but Not too Close
> One very cold night a group of porcupines were huddled together for warmth. However, their spines made proximity uncomfortable so they moved apart again and got cold. After shuffling repeatedly in and out, they eventually found a distance at which they could still be comfortably warm without getting pricked. This distance they henceforth called decency and good manners.
> —A German fable
> (quoted by Edward O. Wilson, 257)

These two incidents are metaphors of at least two ways difficulties come to a congregation. At times the congregation can see difficulties arising and can progressively prepare for honest conflicts that are inevitable. An example would be when some members want to build a new sanctuary and others strongly oppose it. The conflict can be handled in positive ways and the church can be enriched by the decisions that are made. For example small group meetings can be convened to discuss proposed construction with instructions given on how all participants can listen carefully—empathic listening as suggested by Stephen Covey in an earlier chapter of this book. The conflict can be destructive if leaders fail to see it coming and do not plan healthy ways for the members to interact about the decision.

The other type of conflict is the one that hits the congregation broadside without any warning. One example could be the discovery that the treasurer has been using the church's reserve account for her own purposes and now, to compound the matter, she has been released by her employer and is unable to pay back thousands of dollars. Wham! Every member of the congregation soon learns of the problem, and all kinds of suggestions emerge about what actions to take, some of them not very charitable.

This is when the fur flies. I first heard that expression from my dad. He explained to me that when two tom cats get into a fight you can pick up the hair from both cats at the site of their battle. In like manner church conflicts can be fierce and persons can be hurt.

Persons can be offended over actions and words in a church fellowship that would provoke little response at work or school. It is equally true that we all look to the fellowship of the church as a haven from the injuries of the world and are surprised when we are hurt in the fellowship. The persons whom we love most are the persons who can hurt us most. If I meet someone on the street and he calls me "a mean, old, bald-headed, chubby man," I would not be pleased but would laugh it off and probably tell several others about it. If my wife or one of my children said something like that it would really hurt. We anticipate that we will receive love, encouragement, and personal support in our family and in the church and when, if even rarely, something abrasive happens, we need some time to adjust.

Occasionally situations get a bit rough in the fellowship. Occasionally persons who are brothers and sisters in Christ have feelings of resentment and betrayal and are frustrated with one another. Occasionally people in the church act immaturely; some say things they shouldn't say. People are people and, as we shall see in just a moment, even in the early church, leaders and members had to learn to deal with the people factor in the church.

In the Holiness tradition we have at times suggested that when one is filled with the Holy Spirit, sanctified, the carnal nature is eradicated and one never says anything or does anything hurtful again. We have been in error to suggest that becoming a Christian makes one a perfect human being. Every sanctified person relies on the power of the Holy Spirit to live a life that is consistent with being a disciple of Jesus, but every sanctified person has to deal with those human characteristics that can cause conflict with others. At times those who claim to be so humanly perfect are the most insufferable in relationships. In other words, they are really hard to take.

People are people and to expect them to be angels is unrealistic. That they live under grace, have confessed their sins, and have committed themselves to live for Christ is miraculous. Each is on a journey to perfection through the power of the Spirit; few are so perfect that they are not a bother to at least a few others.

Trouble Between the Christians in Corinth

One of the essential instructional manuals for all Christians is the letter Paul wrote to the followers of Christ living in Corinth. He says:

I appeal to you, brothers and sisters, by the name of our Lord Jesus Christ, that all of you be in agreement and that there be no divisions among you, but that you be united in the same mind and same purpose. For it has been reported to me by Chloe's people that there are quarrels among you, my brothers and sisters.
(1 Corinthians 1:10–11)

> **Unhealthy Unity**
> Kerr and Bowen argue that the "one for all and all for one" consensus approach in leadership or in an organization makes for an unhealthy "unity"....
> In fact many emotionally and spiritually weak people do dominate the church.
> They often appear emotionally fragile, and people around them "walk on eggshells." Sometimes they dominate the church with their messages: "Poor me," or "The church is not meeting my needs (or saving my children)."
> But systems theory teaches that the seemingly weak member of a family or a church is the most powerful, organizing everyone around his or her needs.
> —R. Paul Stevens and Phil Collins (33)

One of the arguments of this group of people was about the superiority of Paul or Apollos. Some claimed to be followers of one, the other group of the second leader. Paul would have none of their quarreling and insisted that they consider themselves followers of Christ.

For our purposes here we can note four lessons:

1. Christian people get into arguments in the church over subjects they should not argue over—among them, who is the best, Paul or Apollos, or the current pastor or

the former pastor. People, yes, Christian people, do have disagreements.

2. Christians who will take the time to recall that they are Christ's followers can settle many of their arguments. Consideration of the mission that Christ has entrusted to us enables us to see many controversies as unimportant.

3. Even when a controversy is settled, Paul had to write the Corinthian church again to help members settle other controversial issues. The same is true in our fellowships; we need repeatedly to focus on the person and ministry of Jesus Christ if we are to avoid those trifles that can take our time and destroy the fellowship.

4. People are people and we all must seek the mind of Christ in all situations or the church soon reverts to being just another human institution.

You Can See the Storm Coming

A pastor in his first year with a congregation recently said, "I could see it coming; I knew the subject was going to come up sometime!" The "subject" was waking him up in the middle of the night. He found himself thinking about it when he wanted to pray about other concerns. It occupied his mind when he was driving to and from work or to the hospital for visitation. He saw the storm coming and several persons in the church saw it coming also. Some wanted to face the issue; others were curious about how the pastor would fare on the first major test of his pastoral leadership.

What the situation or subject was doesn't make much difference. In fact, you can choose the subject. Which one of these subjects do you think was causing the pastor and other leaders stress?

- Speaking in tongues.
- Persons required to be good financial stewards if they serve in leadership roles.
- Changes in the bylaws.
- The place of practicing homosexuals in the life of the church.
- The associate pastor who is not working at his or her assigned tasks.
- A new worship style.
- Introduction of the idea of a second Sunday morning worship service.
- Moving the church to a new location.
- Beginning a one-board system of governance.
- A square dance in the fellowship hall.

Each of these subjects can cause members of the congregation to express strong and often contradictory feelings about "what we have always done" and "the will of the Lord." The inference we make is that "my way of thinking" just happens to correspond with what the Lord really wants.

Probably, if a church can wisely deal with a storm that it is able to see coming, then it is equipped to handle those emergency situations when a problem broadsides the congregation without warning. Experience at handling controversy does not make an unhappy event any better, but the practice of dealing in healthy ways with major differences can strengthen a fellowship to deal with the surprise conflicts.

> **Conflict and Leadership**
> "If you keep on biting and devouring each other, watch out or you will be destroyed by each other," Paul said in Galatians 5:15. That day has already come for many local churches because the primary reason for church fights is power politics, pure and simple....
> Survey responses demonstrated that pastors are fired for personal reasons—two Lutherans and one Southern Baptist because they weren't friendly enough; an Independent Baptist due to his wife's attitude; a veteran Wesleyan due to the need for a younger man; and a United Methodist pastor for having children and pets in the parsonage. One Presbyterian pastor listed over involvement beyond the local church as the cause of his departure. In most of these cases internal political problems in the congregation were accompanying factors....
> Warren Weirsbe has written, "I have discovered that the lack of respect for spiritual leadership is the main cause for church fights and splits." Could he be right?
> —Rodney J. Crowell (57, 59–60)

The Way It Is

People will be people but the life of the fellowship may be richer and more effective if we are aware of a few of the dynamics in a group's life. Among those factors in group life are these:

1. Many issues really are not worth an argument. Why argue over the possibility of a second worship service? Experiment with it for six months and if it works, continue the service. If no one attends, stop it. Everyone (well, most people) can agree to experiment. Millions are starving in the world, hundreds in our church neighborhoods do not know Christ, children are turn-

ing to drugs to be accepted, and it does not seem right that the members of the church spend hours debating worship styles, what brand of organ to purchase, or the color scheme of the entrance to the sanctuary. These and many other subjects are important but not worth elevating from a disagreement to a conflict.

2. People bring their dysfunctional family behavior into the church family. Some persons come from families that argue every decision and every subject. Some persons come from abusive families and are fearful of any close relationship. Often persons are behaving in church as they behave at home. Recognizing they are dysfunctional and accepting them can defuse their anger and soothe some feelings of inadequacy.

3. Sometimes in a church meeting what we are talking about is not what we are talking about. A church had invited a young pastor to speak and was considering calling him. The daughter of one of the church leaders asked her dad if he was going to vote for the new pastor. In turn, he asked how another leader of the church was going to vote. His daughter realized her dad was not going to vote for or against the new pastor but was going to vote opposite of the way the other leader voted.

Unfortunately, persons who disagree often are not talking about the subject at hand but are continuing an argument between groups, an argument that has gone on for years. The subject is different but the adversaries remain the same. This may be happening in your church if, repeatedly, otherwise mature and thoughtful persons are divided into two groups on every important issue.

> **Conflict**
> Conflict used to be something that would explode like a volcano in a congregation, with no sense that anything could be done. If you read the future in terms of diversity, then you should realize that conflict is the name of diversity. A church that cares about diversity, and cares about allowing individuality to be expressed, has to learn to deal with conflict.
> —Loren Mead (310)

4. When people strongly disagree on a subject or issue that is important to both, a time of stress is inevitable. We err when we attempt to suppress or disavow the disagreement. We act maturely when we acknowledge the differences and plan for adequate time (weeks or months) to hear each other and to understand each other. It is amazing how persons who sincerely disagree can come to love each other when they sense the other is genuinely interested in what he or she has to say. (You may want to read again Stephen Covey's statement on empathic listening quoted in chapter 2.)

5. Trouble comes when one group in the church has information that is not commonly shared. Disillusionment is inevitable when committees have secret information about proposed building plans, new pastoral leadership, a personal problem emerging in the fellowship, or whatever, and retain that information for themselves. Trouble erupts in relationships when important information is considered the property of a select few. This is a characteristic of a dysfunctional family and also of dysfunctional churches.

6. Competitiveness is a characteristic of our culture and, when it gets into the fellowship of the church, can be destructive. Wayne Oates has identified some sources of this competitiveness. We probably cannot exclude it from the church, for we are a part of a competitive culture; however, we may be able to keep the competitive spirit from reducing church life to a game of winners and losers. Oates has made some suggestions to help us understand competitors in the life of the church:

• Some persons come from families where siblings are highly competitive and they bring that must-win attitude into the fellowship.

• A self-made successful person has developed competitive skills and may see leadership in the church as something to be grasped.

• Families that have long been a part of a local congregation may have rivalries that continue to be fought in the election of leaders and decisions about the budget.

• Pastor-staff members can get into competition for attention, influence, and "who is liked best."

• A pastor who avoids the administrative guidance of a congregation creates a leadership vacuum and other persons take over that leadership, sometimes persons who are not necessarily the choice of the congregation.

• Generations tend to become competitive, vying to see which age-group will control the direction of the church.

• Persons who lose in the competition and are not in roles they wanted in the life of the congregation can be seriously hurt in both their personal lives and in their spiritual development (adapted from Oates, 46–53).

7. The local church has greater possibilities of enduring difficult times of disagreement and conflict if they have agreed on purpose and direction, created in calmer moments. The Church of God created a Task Force on Governance and Polity, which reported to the church in 1992 after five years of study. One message for the local congregation was emphatic:

> We believe that *relationships, not structure*, are the primary key for congregational effectiveness. To accomplish this, we urge the congregations engage in regular, candid and open discussion about mission, ministry and relationships. They will be helped by creating mission, covenant and vision statements. A covenant statement will use the biblical experience of God's covenant with His people as a basis for a statement of relationships and accountability.

You will note that the task force suggests some intense planning (structure?) as a step toward more harmonious relationships as being of paramount importance in the life of the church; structure is important in relationships, but it is a servant, not the master, of relationships, and when structure supersedes relationships congregations begin to have other things and not people as priority.

Pastor Bill Hybels of Willow Creek Church near Chicago says, "Unity isn't the word we use to describe relationships ... we use the word community.... The mark of community—true biblical unity—is not the absence of conflict. It's the presence of a reconciling spirit." Hybels explains that "when your nose gets bent out of joint" you have the responsibility to take "the high road of conflict resolution." Also, when someone wants to talk about the problem they are having with another, it is the member's responsibility to say the discontented one should go talk with the other person involved and resolve the conflict in a "God-glorifying way" (*Leadership*, 1993, 14–15).

That is the way one congregation is doing just what we have been talking about, when the fur flies, or, even better, before the fur flies.

Resurrection

You have to want peace more than war. It is a difficult message for countries and ethnic groups to hear. Differing histories, environments, and standards make the difficulty at times understandable. Within the local church (and the larger church) it is just as important that members renew their commitment to people rather than continue old arguments and retain old animosities, many of them ridiculous, all of them stifling the Spirit and mission of the church.

A beautiful story is told of Father Elias Chacour of Galilee, a pastor of a thriving congregation that has served the community by providing a high school and many other services. As recorded in an interview by Jim Forest, Elias became pastor of the then small congregation several years ago and discovered the building in disrepair with no ministry to the community. The congregation was divided into four groups, each identified to a great extent with one of four brothers. The groups kept their distance and the brothers did not come together even at the time of their mother's death.

On Palm Sunday, in the first year of his pastorate, Elias led the congregation in a worship service and preached to the group of "stony faces," including the brother who was a police officer sitting up front. At the conclusion of the service he surprised himself and the congregation.

Elias padlocked the door, then said:

> Sitting in this building does not make you a Christian. You are a people divided. You argue and hate each other. You gossip and spread lies. Your religion is a lie. If you can't love your brother, whom you can see, how can you say that you love God, who is invisible? You have allowed the Body of Christ to be disgraced. I have tried for months to unite you. I have failed. I am only a man. But there is someone else who can bring you together in true unity. His name is Jesus. He has the power to forgive you. So now I will be quiet and allow him to give you that power. If you will not forgive, then we stay locked in here. If you want, you can kill each other, and I'll provide your funeral gratis.

Time passed, minutes seemed hours. The police officer stood up and said, "I'm sorry. I'm the worst of all. I have hated my own brothers." He asked forgiveness from them and his pastor. Elias embraced the police officer and then encouraged him to embrace his brothers as all three rushed to embrace him. Elias recalls that the building became a "chaos of embracing and repentance."

Elias made another announcement: "We are not going to wait until next week to celebrate the resurrection. Let us begin it now. We were dead to each other. Now we are alive again." They sang hymns and then began to march in the streets. All day believers went from house to house: "At every door, someone had to ask forgiveness for a certain wrong. Never was forgiveness withheld" (Kirkpatrick 15–17).

Such resurrections are happening today in churches. Does your church need such a resurrection from conflict? You probably can have it. All it takes is getting rid of some feelings you don't want, forgiving some words that may not have been that bad in the first place, and reestablishing a relationship with someone you need. Seems like a good deal to me, this resurrection of fellowship through forgiveness.

Ponder and Process

Action Process
Identify a conflict that may be developing in your group. Go to a person who has a different opinion from yours in the matter and ask the person about their viewpoint. Listen.

Meditation Process
Practice words and sentences that will enable you to express your opinion or feelings without starting an argument with another.

Discussion Process
Read 1 Corinthians 1:10–17. Review the four lessons that are identified by this scripture:
1. Christian people argue.
2. Many controversies are unimportant.
3. Repeatedly focus on ministry.
4, People are people; seek the mind of Christ.

State your congregation's mission in one sentence.

State your group's vision for your congregation, again in one sentence.

Discuss how acceptance of the concept of Bill Hybels may improve relationships in your congregation: "Unity isn't the word we use to describe relationships ... we use the word community.... The mark of community—true biblical unity—is not the absence of conflict. It's the presence of a reconciling spirit."

Before praying, read Psalm 139:1–4 or sing the hymn *Cleanse Me*.

> Search me, O God, and know my heart today;
> Try me, O Savior, know my heart, I pray.
> See if there be some wicked way in me;
> Cleanse me from every sin, and set me free.
> —J. Edwin Orr

Chapter 9

THE FREEDOM FACTOR

People need freedom. Freedom is not license to do as we please. It is liberty to live and function within broad parameters. Legalism sets boundaries about everything and prescribes how life shall be lived, as if the directions for life can be as specific as a way to cut a tabletop from a piece of lumber. Freedom is not only permission to think and act within certain broad boundaries; freedom is also the created climate, a climate for personal discovery, decision making, and growth.

The church, as is typical of most groups, tends to develop rules for participation in the fellowship. The church also sees secular pursuits to be a part of the Christian life and thus has rules for life in the secular world. Guidelines, rather than laws or rules, are more acceptable to mature and growing persons. The Bible has some broad basic rules that are a foundation for the Christian life; for example, do not kill and do not steal are specific. Yet, too often Christian fellowships have included rules for dress, hair styles, food, religious practices, and functions in the home, rules created that go beyond the clear instructions of the Word of God.

A question was posed in a small interest group of which I am a member: "Are we accountable to other Christians?" The question triggered negative responses from several in the group. One said, "I had people in the church telling me what I could and could not do when I was a child, through my teen years, and much of my adult life. I don't want any more of their restrictions and legalisms." Religious bondage has been for some just as debilitating as bondage to sin. In a subsequent discussion our group agreed that guidelines and support are very helpful in a Christian fellowship but an abundance of rules, which may be used in a very legal way, turns the joy of the Christian life into drudgery and stress. Carrying a cross in Jesus' name is essentially different from carrying crosses imposed by a group or, more often, by a few persons in a group.

Irreducible Disciplines of the Faith
Reverence for God: Psalm 95:1–7
Respect for persons: Matthew 22:37–40
Salvation and sanctification: 1 John 1:5–9
 and Romans 12:1–2
Generosity: 2 Corinthians 8:2–7
Accountability: Ephesians 5:15–21
Maturity: Hebrews 6:1–2
Joy: Philippians 4:4–7
—from *Withrow, Hi-Q Christians*

The first church fellowships were reminded of the freedom factor in the letters of Paul. He instructed the Corinthians, "Now the Lord is the Spirit, and where the

Spirit of the Lord is, there is freedom" (2 Corinthians 3:17). The statement follows a comparison of the legal limitations of the Mosaic law to the liberating transformation for those who are in Christ. The verse, however, has meaning and impact far beyond its scriptural context. The text, for instance, has been on the name plate of the *Indianapolis Star* for decades, in the King James Version—"Where the Spirit of the Lord is, there is liberty." It is an adequate guide for the local church, reminding each fellowship that freedom (or liberty) is characteristic of the fellowship of Christians.

> **Freedom Is a Climate**
> Freedom is more than a permission to do something, it is creating and sustaining a climate, an atmosphere, that encourages and enables growth and maturity. It is not a license for irresponsibility or immorality, it is latitude, an openness to many good options. Freedom in Christ is an emancipation from sin and religious legalism so that the individual believer and the group may live as thoughtful servants, not as programmed robots.

The question about responsible use of freedom is addressed by Paul. He had previously spoken of a religious/cultural prohibition on eating meat offered to idols. He suggests that he sees no wrong in eating the meat but advises that if eating it causes offense to another believer then he would choose not to do so (1 Corinthians 8). Even this can become a legalism as persons are coerced into certain behavior patterns, on the basis that their actions may be offensive to someone. Such is not the intent of this scripture.

One person expressed to a group, "If you go to a movie and that offends me, then you are obligated not to go to that movie." The twisting of the scripture makes it a manipulative tool so that one can force others to live by his or her conscience. Paul was seeking to free, not restrict, people. The law of God and meticulous obedience to Mosaic interpretations of the law are different things. Jesus summarized the law in two parts: reverence the Lord and respect people. Individuals and congregations are encouraged with Paul's words to the Christians in Galatia: "For freedom Christ has set us free. Stand firm, therefore, and do not submit again to a yoke of slavery" (Galatians 5:1). It is an integral concern of every congregation that freedom in Christ be maintained. Paul expands the concept of freedom, insisting that the common practice of circumcision does not count for anything; "the only thing that counts is faith working through love" (Galatians 5:6). Both Paul and the Apostle Peter warned of the abuse of freedom. Paul said:

> For you were called to freedom, brothers and sisters; only do not use your freedom as an opportunity for self-indulgence, but through love become slaves to one another.
>
> (Galatians 5:13)

Peter expressed the same principle in one of his letters to the first Christians: "As servants of God, live as free people, yet do not use your freedom as a pretext for evil" (1 Peter 2:16).

While congregations must focus on what it is to be "in Christ," a lot of freedom, including the freedoms we will suggest, is essential to a vital and healthful congregation.

Freedom to Forgive

The freedom to forgive seems so obvious and one might say, "If you want to forgive, go ahead and forgive." In practice it is not so easily done.

Forgiveness requires conversation. In one of my relationships I earnestly desired a reconciliation and mutual forgiveness but found in my Christian friend no willingness to converse about the matter. Forgiveness includes a mutual commitment to a higher cause or purpose, such as to uphold the name of Christ or the reputation of the church; but it is possible to have a commitment to remembering and not forgetting a wrong. Forgiveness requires an openness to the conviction and guidance of the Holy Spirit, but resentment and bitterness can distort divine signals that urge reconciliation.

The expectations of family and friends, within the fellowship of the church, may hinder a person's initiative to forgive or seek forgiveness. One father said to his son, "If you ever let them forget that, I'll have little respect for you." A Christian friend, though I think one who is out of line, encouraged the continuation of a ruined relationship by suggesting, "Tell them that if that person participates in the service, you won't." Not everyone is at a level of spiritual maturity that he or she can tolerate someone else forgiving a person. The spiritually immature involve themselves in others' relationships and, for some reason, the conflict of others is tied in with their own ego needs. Then, too, some persons prefer controversy; having quarreled in their family since childhood, they seek out persons who are "wrong" to work and talk against; they find interest in life through disagreements and sustained conflict.

My unforgiving relationship with a friend, even another Christian, may be encouraged by persons very dear to me, and if I seek or express forgiveness it will jeopardize my treasured relationship with my loved one. Such is not appropriate in the church and platitudes may offer easy ways to get around these friends and relatives but, nonetheless, it is not a positive climate for forgiveness.

Holding on to resentments provides good excuses and a ready reason for selective participation. If Jim (obviously not his name) does not forgive Tom for what Tom once said about Jim's dad, then Jim has an excuse for avoiding meetings where Tom is present and for giving very little money to the church because Tom is an elder. Jim also won't grow spiritually because he refuses to honor any group that would accept Tom as a member. Jim may be blind to the fact that he can participate in another fellowship where Tom is not present, but that would take away all of his excuses. Perhaps most of us are not so hard-set in our resentment over a thoughtless word or action, but we all are tempted to use soured relationships as a vehicle for exempting ourselves from mature behavior and involvement with the group.

The freedom to forgive is established in a congregation when leaders, including the pastor, openly forgive each other in ways that demonstrate that forgiveness is difficult but essential to personal faith and the health of the church.

The freedom to forgive is established in scripture; guidance is given on practical ways to heal differences between Christians:

1. Go to the person who has offended you or whom you have offended and seek reconciliation.
2. If the person is not reconciled and differences settled, then take two or three respected spiritual leaders and speak with the estranged person.
3. If the second effort is not successful, then take the matter to a responsible church leadership group (elders, for instance) and seek advice in settling the issue.
(Matthew 18:15–20)

Often the first step is not taken and differences are permitted to stew and breed an increasingly foul relationship that affects the total fellowship. Rarely does one hear of congregational leaders who care enough to take the risk of being conciliators and arbiters in estranged relationships. Instead, most leaders choose not to get involved with something "that is between them." Leaders would enhance the church's ministry if they were willing to take the risk.

Freedom to forgive means establishing a pattern to accept forgiveness. We have previously spoken about grace. Jeanine may sustain a wrong relationship with Sally because Jeanine has not accepted forgiveness for her sins. One ministry of the church is to help persons accept forgiveness for past sins. This enables Jeanine also to accept the forgiveness of Sally.

Receiving forgiveness is often just as difficult as granting it. Forgiving someone and receiving forgiveness means that I become vulnerable to being misunderstood again, hurt again, overreacting again, losing my temper again. The refusal to participate in a forgiving relationship means that I remain tense. I watch every word and action, lest something I say or do be interpreted wrongly. I thus lose the freedom to flow in the fellowship, relating to everyone with ease and grace. The price of forgiveness and forgiving is great but the cost of not forgiving and for not accepting forgiveness is devastating. Any medical doctor can tell us that harboring anger and resentment produces emotional and physical illnesses; worse yet, estranged relationships produce spiritual callousness, guilt, and condemnation.

Freedom to forgive means establishing situations and opportunities for exercising forgiveness. Sermons on forgiveness can be concluded with an invitation to go to someone that day, perhaps even at that moment, and seek and offer forgiveness. My son-in-law tells of an experience when he felt great conviction over the way he reacted to a couple who left the church he pastored to go to another congregation. Three years later one Sunday morning he tried to contact them before they went to their church but could not reach them by telephone. He was going to preach on a subject related to his own confession of wrong and wanted to tell them he was sorry. He gave up on contacting them and went to the place of worship to preach. As he entered the building the family was standing in the hall, though they had not been to a worship service in the church he pastored for months. He asked why they were there and they explained that for some reason they were impressed to come. He told them he was wanting to say he was sorry, and they explained that they wanted to apologize also. In addition to the other good things that happened, the pastor and laypersons found the climate of forgiveness much healthier than the climate of resentment and distrust.

> **Close the Circle**
> Then we can tell you something else. All humans are spirits only visiting this world. All spirits are forever beings. All encounters with other people are experiences, and all experiences are forever connections. Real People close the circle of each experience. We do not leave ends frayed as Mutants do. If you walk away with bad feelings in your heart for another person and that circle is not closed, it will be repeated later in your life. You will not suffer once but over and over until you learn. It is good to observe, to learn, and become wiser from what has happened. It is good to give thanks, as you say, to bless it, and walk away in peace.
> —Marlo Morgan (93)
> —An Australian Aboriginal is speaking.
> Aboriginese consider themselves "Real People" and all others are "Mutants"

Freedom to forgive is established as small groups are created for fellowship and nurture. Persons can confess their need for help in a circle of friends and find guidance for seeking and offering forgiveness. The support of a covenant small group of Christians strengthens a resolution to restore disturbed relationships.

Freedom to forgive creates a community of God's people that becomes a model for reconciliation for the world. Guidelines for such a community were developed by the late Samuel Hines, pastor of the Third Street Church of God in Washington, DC, and are a part of chapter two, "Ways to Keep People First."

Freedom for a Variety of Spiritual Experiences

Christian congregations encourage each person to have a conversion experience. Also, congregations encourage each person to make a commitment to be a disciplined member of a local congregation. Most groups anticipate that members will have occasional times of inspiration. Christian groups also tend to draw circles (circumscribe) and indicate what experiences are normal and which ones are questionable. Out of fear of something bad happening, congregations may prevent a very good thing from happening.

Not all spiritual experiences are normative, that is, everyone should have them. I do not speak in tongues, as some Christians do. It is appropriate for them to have the experience if it is given by the Holy Spirit, but it is not scriptural to insist that others have that experience.

Some persons indicate they have very precise and clear instructions from the Lord on many subjects and on many occasions. Jeannette is a dear friend who now lives in Tupelo, Mississippi, assisting in the planting of a new congregation. When I was her pastor and often since when Jeannette converses about a decision she may say, "The Lord said to me" or "The Lord told me" and she does not mean that her experience is an impression or a thought. She believes the Lord communicates to her consciousness. Jeannette and I have had a laugh or two when I responded, "Jeannette, it is of no use for me to think or pray about this if the Lord has already told you what is best." Jeannette's maturity and grace keep her from insisting that her spiritual experience is normative, that is, everyone else has to hear from the Lord in the same way, though she is very confident of her own directions from the Lord.

Jesus spoke of the mystery of spiritual experiences when he explained the miracle of being born again: "The wind blows where it chooses, and you hear the sound of it, but you do not know where it comes from or where it goes. So it is with everyone who is born of the Spirit" (John 3:8).

You will want to read Robert Reitz's report on a special spiritual experience, "Routine Transformed by Divine Experience" (see next page). Bob has been a civic and church leader, and when he told me of the meaning of this experience to him, I was touched. Even an experience like Bob's, though at once simple and beautiful, cannot be normative; it may help another Christian be more open to unusual inspiration.

A community of believers has a noticeable vitality when it seeks to discover the variety of ways members are experiencing God in their lives. One could say that this may reduce the Christian experience to a purely subjective interpretation—that is, whatever we experience is valid and our Christian walk is thus defined by the sum of our experiences. It would be an error to do that, of course, for the Bible is the authority on the Christian experience. It identifies the essential spiritual

Routine Transformed by Divine Assurance

As a part of my daily routine I started walking around our neighborhood lake. Bob Reardon and I met and began conversation as we walked. We spoke of how great the day was—beautiful, warm, sunny. Bob said that he had just returned from northern Indiana and noticed the beautiful countryside and peaceful towns as he drove. Bob said, "Everyone should know that there is more to life than the crime, violence, and racial hatred that we see all the time on television." We continued to focus our thoughts and conversation on how good God had been to us and our families.

I mentioned to Bob that I was feeling like a real "has been." Retirement from active business and civic affairs changed my lifestyle drastically. With those thoughts uppermost in my mind, I returned home for breakfast and preparation for church. For my devotions I turned to the book of Revelation.

Unexpectedly a powerful thought came to my mind: "I may be a 'has been' as far as business and civic affairs, but I don't need to be a 'has been' in my Christian pilgrimage." The promises of heaven leaped from the scriptures, and I was caught up in an unusual worship experience. I rededicated my life to Christ and asked Him for a new infilling of His Spirit. Shortly after, I left for church feeling unusually good!

Gilbert Stafford, speaker for Christians Broadcasting Hope, was visiting preacher for our congregation that Sunday. His sermon title was "Living on the Edge" and his text from Revelation. I thought, "I just read these same scriptures at home." Early in the sermon Gil said, "Everyone—every man, every woman, every boy, and every girl should know there is more to life than crime, violence, and racial hatred we see around us."

I couldn't help but be surprised at the words, identical words to those Bob Reardon and I had used just hours before.

Gil reminded us that we are "living on the edge." We are promised a heavenly reward but we aren't there yet. He urged us to rededicate our lives to Christ and seek an infilling of His Spirit. I thought, "This is really for me. I just had that experience two hours ago in my home." I really felt God was affirming me and confirming my experience.

Gil read again from the scripture: "He will wipe away every tear from their eyes, and death shall be no more, neither shall there be mourning nor crying nor pain any more, for the former things have passed away." The fact is, we aren't there yet—we are "living on the edge." We still face pain and suffering.

Again my thoughts and commitments were reaffirmed. My sister-in-law had just returned from cancer surgery. Jean and I were going right from church to take the noon meal to her. Yes, we are "living on the edge" but we have Christ to guide us even in times of ill health.

It was all a wonderful worship experience. I hope that I'll be in tune again for another blessing, another day. —Robert Reitz experiences such as repentance, new birth, Spirit infilling, divine guidance, commitment to cross carrying, and discipleship. Experiences that negate or ignore the biblical guidelines are questionable.

Even so, latitude is important in the fellowship. Persons experience God differently, even within the boundaries clearly stated in the Bible. Many persons are freed to experience God in ways that are personally edifying when prompted by the testimony of another. The one reporting a spiritual experience, careful not to make his or her experience the standard for everyone, may indicate, "Here is how I met God in my life."

In the life of the church we discourage freedom when we prescribe all experiences, because then all experiences will be the same. Rather, we describe how God has met persons in their lives, particularly when their experiences have a ring of authenticity. It is possible that older theological forms of experiencing the divine may be broken (or bent), but theology is at its best when it enables and encourages persons to express what God is doing through them and how God is relating to them.

Truth is, my spiritual experiences have not always corresponded with what I believed at the time. Spiritual experiences are transforming. When spiritual experiences become packaged, completely defined, and acceptable only if identical to those of a previous generation, then we restrict the creativity of the Holy Spirit and the adventure of the believer. Consider two churches.

Prairie Community Church often includes the testimony of a layperson in the worship services, sometimes with an interview format. The music on Sunday morning includes hymns and choruses led by a five-member worship group and has a choir that sings on some Sundays and presents special programs for Christmas and Easter. Nearly half of the adult members are a part of a small group; most groups meet one hour each week for fellowship, prayer, and Bible study. The leader of the group often pastors members of the group during times of illness or family stress.

Many members are involved in leadership in Prairie Church. Task forces are created with specific assignments and cease to exist when the task is completed. The leadership of the pastor encourages the congregation to explore and experiment with ministries. Members have a high trust level and are vulnerable; it is not unusual for them to laugh about a mistake they made last year or a program that flopped. Missions projects sponsored through their annual Faith Promise Convention are suggested by the members who are involved in missions studies and work camps.

The previous religious experiences of members are respected and honored. Though Prairie Church practices believer's baptism, it lets each person who has been baptized as an infant decide whether and when to be rebaptized. A couple who were formerly members of a church that baptized infants came to the pastor with a problem: they now believed in baptism after conversion but their parents, the grandparents of their baby, were requesting that the baby be baptized. The pastor suggested that the grandparents could help plan an infant baptism that would be consistent with their faith and also be invited as honored guests to an infant dedication service, which was now more consistent with the parents' belief.

Prairie Community Church is a congregation that is relaxing and enjoying its faith and fellowship.

First Church, by comparison, is holding on. The pastor and a few other selected persons have all the speaking parts in the worship services. The order and elements of the worship service are so predictable that even when minor changes occur they are announced as evidence of variety. The pastor and a few lay leaders are in control. Areas of responsibility are guarded. Recently, a few members wanted to experiment with an outreach ministry and were told that a committee existed for that purpose and it would be best to write up their suggestion and send a copy to the pastor. Groups in the church are protective of ways of worship, certain furniture and classrooms, and traditions.

During worship most of the members know when to stand and sit and know when they are expected to have the correct page for a hymn or reading. One mystery to a person who recently became a member is how the older members of the congregation know when it is appropriate to applaud and when it is not; persons who applaud at the wrong time feel obvious and alone. Though previous religious experiences are appreciated, all members are expected to be saved, sanctified, and baptized in the accepted pattern. It is made known that certain experiences are not recognized and that expressions of praise are to be restrained. As indicated, Prairie Church is hanging loose and First Church is holding on.

Both Prairie Church and First Church are composites of several churches but they are valid descriptions. It is a part of my present assignment to study and visit with congregations to help them discover their future, and I find that each congregation more nearly fits into either the model of Prairie Church or First Church. Which description more nearly describes your local church? Is it nearer to Prairie Church or to First Church?

More freedoms essential in a dynamic Christian fellowship are identified in the next chapter.

Ponder and Process

Action Process

Give a person who is dear to you more freedom—allow the person to freely express how she feels about your relationship and what her dreams are. It could be a member of your family, a close friend, or a member of the church whom you wish would do things differently.

Meditation Process

Think for five minutes about a freedom from legalism you would like to have in your own life. You could think about just one freedom that would liberate you or make a list of several freedoms you seek in your spiritual or church life.

Discussion Process

Select three persons to read scripture portions: Galatians 5:13–14; 1 Peter 2:16–17; 2 Corinthians 3:17.

Inquire if any have done the Action Process or thought through the suggestions for the Meditation Process. Ask, "Do you have any insights to share?"

Identify beliefs and practices you have in your congregation that are nonnegotiable, irreducible.

List two beliefs and practices in your congregation that are primarily the concern of a few but not of most members of the congregation.

In brief form, tell your class or small group of an unexpected or unusual personal spiritual experience.

Prayer: Ask persons to name a freedom in the church for which they are thankful.

Following each person's statement, lead the group in the response, "Thank you, Lord!"

Conclude prayer by saying, "And all God's people said, Amen."

Chapter 10

MORE ON FREEDOM

Freedom is essential in the life of the church; individual Christians and the local Christian fellowship can flourish in freedom. Remember freedom is more than permission to do what one wants; it is creating and sustaining a climate that encourages and enables growth. Two freedoms were identified in the previous chapter: freedom to forgive and freedom for a variety of spiritual experiences.

Six more freedoms characteristic of a biblically-based fellowship and a caring community of believers are these:

- Freedom to know and accept
- Freedom for ministry
- Freedom to decide, to choose, without coercion
- Freedom within the fellowship
- Freedom of conscience
- Freedom to be a pilgrim

The freedom to know each other includes a responsibility to know the other person and the joy of having the other person know us in more than a superficial way. Otherwise, we both operate on the basis of prejudice in our relationship. Prejudice blocks freedom. Prejudice is a negative opinion or judgment that is decided upon before all facts are considered; it is a preconceived conviction about persons. In an effort to overcome prejudice, Coach Lou Tepper of the University of Illinois football team informs all recruits that team members will relate on an interracial basis. Each player rooms with someone of a different race during training and on the road. At the evening training-table meal players sit with persons other than close friends on the team. In the locker room a poster reads, "Prejudice is a great time saver: it enables you to form an opinion of others without bothering to get the facts."

Every member of a congregation deserves to be known; this requires effort and time. It is not fair for one person to say unilaterally that another needs to "know me"; knowing others is a mutual responsibility and it frees each of us to be honest, transparent, and trusting. Lest we misunderstand, freedom to know and accept each other is not a license for us to say, "That is just the way I am and you have to accept me!" A statement of that sort indicates an expectation that everyone else will adjust to our quirks or lack of discipline.

People are different. That is a truism but Paul takes great pains to highlight the fact in the spiritual realm, telling us that we have spiritual gifts that differ according to the wisdom of the Spirit and the ministry needs of the church (Romans 12, 1 Corinthians 12, Ephesians 4). Religious groups are prone to forget the beauty of diversity and create belief statements and organizations that bring us into conformity. Covenant relationships are essential disciplines for each Christian, but restrictive limitations are not consistent with the unique qualities of each personality.

> ### Unity/Diversity
> "In Christ we who are many form one body, and each member belongs to all the others" (Romans 12:5). Paul's systemic statement about the church holds in dynamic tension two essential dimensions of the church: unity (togetherness) and the unique existence and function of each member (diversity). When these are dynamically balanced the church functions fruitfully in a life-giving way to its members and the world. But unity without diversity leads to the formation of a monolithic organization, a sect that swallows up the individuality of its members ... diversity without unity leads to rampant individualism and the loss of corporate life. The church would then be merely a bouquet of individual believers ... when unity and diversity are held together in dynamic tension, we experience body life, and the church functions as a healthy, interdependent system.
> —R. Paul Stevens and Phil Collins (20–21)

One pastor and the leadership board repeatedly found themselves strongly differing on the handling of opportunities and problems in the life of the church. They agreed to a longer than usual meeting and each person completed The *Keirsey Temperament Sorter*, a brief form of *The Myers-Briggs Type Indicator*. It is an enjoyable way, and in most cases nonthreatening way, to identify personality differences. Instructions for the use of this personality indicator are in the book *Please Understand Me: Character Temperament Types* by David Keirsey and Marilyn Bates. Another book that is very helpful to pastors and lay leaders is *Personality Type and Religious Leadership* by Roy M. Oswald and Otto Kroeger. The books and forms may be ordered from Life Structure Resources, PO Box 212, Boonsboro, Maryland 21713; telephone 800-723-0625.

When the pastor and the lay leaders completed their personality inventories and discussed how their differences make them see possibilities and problems from different perspectives they began to enjoy differences and accept each other. Of course, one or two persons may continue to think their way of seeing things is the only rational or mature or spiritual way to view life, but most persons will welcome the opportunity to understand why a very dear friend repeatedly has a different perspective on responsibilities, entertainment, and many other subjects.

One of my associate pastors of several years ago was a person whom I loved and who loved me, but at times we failed to communicate. One reason was our distinct personality traits. Using the *Keirsey Sorter* indicators for personality type we became aware that I was an ENTJ and Darrell was an INTP. The last letter of our types was the key to what made our working relationship problematic. You see *J* indicates one who meets deadlines and expects everyone else to do so. *P* indicates that a person hesitates to come to any final decision on any issue, keeps options open, and may use a deadline as a reminder to start working on the task. People are different, as were my associate and I, but cooperative and creative efforts can result as persons accept the differences and know the adjustments each will have to make to have an effective group. My associate and I both wish we had worked a little harder on understanding each other.

The task of knowing and accepting each other takes time, but the time involved is very rewarding and encouraging. It is rewarding not only to learn more about the other person but to understand ourselves better. Laura and I took the inventory several years ago. She experienced great freedom as she discovered it is entirely appropriate to be an introvert and that introverts, a minority of the population, are perfectly acceptable people. It made her feel good as she discovered that both introverts and extroverts can serve with their unique gifts and personalities.

Dozens of personality indicators exist and have different values. The *Keirsey Temperament Sorter* is rather easy to use with minimal training while several others require extensive training and time for use with a group. Another simple form is *Personality Plus*, which seeks to help us understand others by understanding ourselves. Florence Littauer uses a popular model for discussing personality types, a model that includes the following categories:

- Sanguine
- Melancholy
- Choleric
- Phlegmatic

She indicates the strengths of each type and adjustments each type may have to make in a group. A personality profile and scoring sheet is included in the book available in many book stores (Florence Littauer, *Personality Plus*, Grand Rapids, Michigan: Fleming H. Revell, a Division of Baker Book House, revised 1992).

Other ways of knowing each other are suggested in chapter 2, "How to Put People First." If we know each other we find a wonderful freedom in worship and ministry. We can relate to each other having taken the time and made the effort to overcome prejudices—prejudices which are a problem in any group.

Freedom for Ministry

Freedom for Ministry involves at least three congregational disciplines:

1. A congregational discipline to help members discover their own gifts and place for ministry in the life of the church.

2. A congregational discipline to focus on ministry rather than organizational structure.

3. A congregational discipline to use only inspiration, information, challenge, and requests as methods for making a person aware of ministry opportunities and needs, refusing to coerce persons or put them on a guilt trip to get them to accept an assignment.

Too often congregations persuade persons to accept positions on boards or committees and devote hours to programs and processes with which they are not familiar.

A person is encouraged to accept the appointment or election because of an organizational need, on the premise that "someone has to do it." The calling, concerns, and gifts of the individual are often given secondary consideration. Persons who accept positions within the organization are considered cooperative members.

The result is that a person will invest all discretionary time in the organizational "slot" and leave little or no time for the ministry about which he or she is concerned. We all can affirm that the organization does need attention so that it may serve as a structure for ministry. The danger is that the organization becomes a sponge that absorbs available personnel to the point that creative ministries are not possible. (See the chapter on "The Time Factor" for additional perspectives on this subject.)

Members can be freed for ministry if they insist that ministry is the first priority. Members are then given guidelines on ways their ministries may be incorporated in the life of the church. A set of guidelines could include these statements:

- Any member may inaugurate a ministry that is a service to persons who have needs.

- The member who has concern for the ministry is the person who is responsible to enlist others to minister with them. An inability to enlist others may indicate the timing isn't right or the person doing the enlisting may need to become better informed about the proposed ministry or the person with the concern may need a better understanding of relational and enlistment skills.

- The new ministry will obtain initial financial support from the persons who share in the ministry without encouraging transfer giving from other ministries of the church.

- The new ministry will demonstrate need and effectiveness for one year before being considered for recognition as a ministry of the congregation.

> **Laypeople Planning and Carrying on Ministry**
> Our concern is to discern God's moving in our church and to get in step with Him. If we have to wait six or ten years for a ministry to begin, that's okay. But when God moves people, our structure must not be in the way.
> A basic assumption in this approach to ministry is that lay people are capable of planning and carrying on a ministry.... But once the priority is established we must then pursue structure diligently.... We need to know, for example, who is responsible, what the objectives are, what physical resources are needed, who is going to supply them.
> —Frank Tillapaugh, (*Unleashed,* 76)

Perhaps the above statements are too restrictive. It is essential that uninformed and undisciplined persons be discouraged from starting projects to which they give only temporary or inadequate attention. It is also important that persons with a concern for ministry be encouraged in their work rather than put through a gauntlet of approval by several boards or committees. Getting approval can be the most discouraging process for any creative idea. Creative people often give up when they have to prove the validity of an idea over and over again. It is amazing to hear the number of questions that can be asked by established boards about a ministry proposal; it is possible to become discouraged with the process for approval and let the concept die.

Pastor Milton Grannum of a fast-growing congregation in Philadelphia insists that members must be free to discover ministry. The Bear Valley Church near Denver has operated for years on a model that encourages its members to discover and create new ministries (books by Frank Tillapaugh, *The Church Unleashed* and *Unleashing Your Potential,* explain the open ministry plan of the Bear Valley congregation). These pastors encourage both a diversity in ministry by members and the ministries remaining connected to the body.

I must confess the churches I have pastored have tended to make it difficult for persons to start new ministries except through persistent presentation to boards and committees (probably in part as a result of my leadership). The church of which I am now a lay member also has a structure that requires approval from several different persons before a ministry may be launched. It is my observation that most of us are ready for a change. Our fear of bad things happening has robbed us of the vision of wonderful things happening as we trust members.

Freedom to Decide, to Choose, without Coercion

Each person needs freedom to make decisions about involvement in all aspects of church life. Some need more ebb and flow to their involvement and must often retreat from intense situations, while others look for additional responsibilities and thrive on problem solving. The ones who must measure out their involvement need recovery time. They may not make long-term commitments to any task. The reason may be personality traits, family situations, or health restrictions. Persons who are more reserved need encouragement from the body to participate at levels consistent with their personality and circumstances. Getting out of one's comfort zone with tasks and in relationships is often helpful and enables growth and adventure. Constantly operating out of one's comfort zone, however, is (dis)stressful. The definition of stress by Archibald Hart quoted previously is repeated here.

Stress

Anything—pleasant or unpleasant—that arouses your adrenaline system and mobilizes your body for "fight or flight," then doesn't let up and allow time for recovery can predispose you to stress disease. Your body simply adapts to living in a constant state of emergency—and you feel no discomfort until damaging results occur.

—Archibald D. Hart (30)

During a church council meeting Charles recommended that John be asked to serve on a group planning for the Homecoming Weekend. Charles explained that John has to be begged and almost forced to do anything, but he volunteered to get John to do it, because "John needs it." Perhaps not all well-intentioned persons like Charles are quite so obvious in taking over someone else's life, but when leaders assume that everyone needs multiple activities, they have failed to understand people and have taken the prerogative each of us has to make decisions for ourselves.

Every congregation boasts many members who know

what others should do. At times even pastors have been known to assume the arrogant role of making decisions for members, not as an adviser but as one who knows best. Laypersons and pastors have been known to coerce persons to stay with a congregation when the persons should have the freedom to choose another group.

Encouragement, persuasion, request, and challenge are valid ways for mature Christians to enlist other Christians for ministries. These simple straightforward methods allow for and encourage participation. Demanding, legislating, insisting, coercing, and manipulating persons take choice out of the hands of the one person who can make the wisest choice. Members are due respect and must be sustained in their freedom to choose and decide.

Freedom within the Fellowship

The fellowship of a local congregation is meant to be inclusive. Restrictions can develop as various groups develop an identity. Some groups of members may develop a sense of ownership of a congregation and newer persons realize they are not "in." Wise leaders recognize this is a familiar temptation. A function of church leaders is to make efforts to include all members in fellowship and in leadership. The task is not easy because even in the church human beings demand territorial rights. The temptation to protect those rights is strong, however unchristian.

Social categories are created by economics, education, tradition, personal popularity, among other ways. These categories invade Christian fellowships. The Apostle

James warned the first Christian groups about the dangers of favoritism within the fellowship:

> If a person with gold rings and in fine clothes comes into your assembly, and if a poor person in dirty clothes also comes in, and if you take notice of the one wearing the fine clothes and say, "Have a seat here, please," while to the one who is poor you say, "Stand there," or "Sit at my feet," have you not made distinctions among yourselves and become judges with evil thoughts?
> (James 2:2–4)

Persons who are wealthy (or wealthier) may be given recognition and a voice in congregational matters even when their stewardship practices are questionable. The presumption is that persons who have money are more intelligent, wiser, and therefore probably have the potential to be more spiritual. Such presumptions are, of course, full of errors. But strata within the fellowship can develop in relation to accomplishments in the secular world.

Titles are a subtle way of inhibiting freedom in fellowship. It occurred to me as a pastor several years ago that I put a noticeable stress on the title of, for instance, medical doctors and college professors, when announcing their participation in the life of the congregation. I also began to notice that pastors were more excited when talking about the addition of a doctor, lawyer, professor, government official, or prominent athlete to the membership of their churches than they were about more common people.

In the fellowship of the church if one has a place of honor because of wealth, another is referred to with a title indicating a level of education, and another is respected because of a political position, lines are being drawn between Christian brothers and sisters. I decided that I would refer to doctors in our fellowship in the same way as other persons, by first name. The doctors, and other persons of similar standing in the community, responded well to the leveling of the fellowship by abandoning the overuse of titles in the church. It is inappropriate for persons who have academic degrees to expect their educational credentials to repeatedly be acknowledged in the fellowship of the church. It is my conviction that many pastors with doctorates would be wiser not to repeatedly use the "Dr." before their name in church bulletins and publications and certainly not refer to themselves with the title. I am aware there are additional social implications in the use of earned and honorary titles for pastors in some cultures, but in many churches the use of such titles has tended to create barriers that are not consistent with the principles of Christian fellowship.

Certainly the concern here is not for an egalitarian fellowship where everyone is presumed to have equal gifts, equal voice, equal vote, equal leadership, and so forth; the biblical lessons on spiritual gifts would void such a concept. The appeal is for a genuine open fellowship in the life of the church that is not blocked by secular positions or titles.

All persons within a fellowship can have the freedom to relate to all other persons in the fellowship as a brother or sister in the Lord. Removing some traditional barriers may help us realize a simple fellowship again.

Persons who have great difficulty with inferiority complexes, who suffer with social limitations, or who have not had the opportunity of graduate education are greatly encouraged as they relate freely to persons who have no such limitations. Freedom to participate fully in the fellowship is wonderful when it happens. Churches can make it happen.

> **Our Group**
> In short, by basing our identity on our social standing, we have become concerned only for our own groups, our own convictions, our own ministries, or simply ourselves. "When we worship the holiness of our own convictions instead of our holy Lord," Oswald Chambers warns, "there is an element in human nature that makes us all possible popes and intolerant upholders of our personal views."
> —John Seel (in Guinness and Seel 72–73)

Freedom of Conscience

Several matters have been identified as conscience questions throughout the history of the church. The question raised in the Corinthian church had to do with whether it was appropriate for a Christian to eat meat that had been presented as an offering in idol worship and then made available on the market. The question had to do with whether the meat was tainted in a spiritual way. Paul said that it did not bother him to eat it, but he would not want to discourage any believer whom it might bother. He indicated, as discussed earlier, that the concern for another's conscience should not become a way of manipulating:

For why should my liberty be subject to the judgment of someone else's conscience? If I partake with thankfulness, why should I be denounced because of that for which I give thanks? So, whether you eat or drink, or whatever you do, do everything for the glory of God.

(1 Corinthians 10:29b–31)

Meat offered to idols is not a problem for most churches today, but many decisions and choices fit into the conscience category. In one national election several religious leaders indicated that "Christians will vote against Kennedy because he will make the Roman Catholic faith our national religion." Many felt their statement was an unnecessary intrusion in a matter of conscience. Of course an identification of our nation with Catholicism did not happen, but the point is that in the United States we have traditionally said that voting in elections is a matter of conscience not to be usurped by a directive from the church. Recently a person expressed to me that he could not understand how a Christian could vote for one candidate because of his stand on an issue. I did not tell my friend that I had voted for the candidate he criticized.

Conscience questions have been the source of some humorous episodes in the history of our church group, and we are no different from other groups in this regard. Shum Benson is my wife's grandfather. In the early 1900s an evangelist came through the hill country of eastern Mississippi teaching that the wearing of neckties was not appropriate (along with suggestions about appropriate adornment for women). Shum Benson removed his necktie because he was a Sunday school teacher and a principal lay leader of the country church at Dixon.

A few years later other preachers let it be known that the "necktie" controversy had died down and they were wearing ties again. Shum continued to wear his white shirt buttoned at the collar with no necktie saying, "I didn't think it made any sense when they said not to wear them and I don't think it makes any difference that I don't wear one. Anyway, someone might come through again preaching against neckties and if they do I won't have to make any changes." Going uptown for Shum was usually going into Philadelphia, Mississippi, and everyone there knew he was "a mighty fine man," necktie or no necktie.

Shum was buried in the 70s with his white shirt buttoned at the top and no necktie—just as it was when he taught Sunday school on Sundays at Pine Grove Church of God in Dixon.

Pastor Tom Howland of Kearney, Nebraska, recounted another episode from the no-necktie era that took place in his state. The ministers and churches were about equally divided on the necktie controversy but the no-necktie people were really giving the others some trouble as their annual camp meeting convened—they were saying that the necktie attracted undue attention to the person and was not appropriate for a Christian.

One night two or three of the no-necktie ministers were on the platform when a pastor wearing a necktie stood to preach. The pastor with the necktie bent over and picked up the large western hat of a no-necktie fellow and placed it on his head. He then walked to the pulpit and sauntered about for a few minutes with the large hat on his head. Soon the camp meeting congregation was laughing without the preacher having to state his point: large hats call much more attention to a person than neckties.

> ### Religion and Politics
> If the role of the religionist is first to make up his or her mind about which political position to take and next to search for religious arguments to support the already selected view, the idea of faith as the source of moral inspiration is trivialized.
> Religions are moral forces in the lives of their adherents, which means, inevitably, that they are moral forces in the political world. And, as with all institutions, a degree of cross-pollination between religion and politics is inevitable. But when secular political considerations become prior to, rather than subsequent to, religious considerations, the result is not cross-pollination but pollution.
> —Stephen L. Carter (81)

The controversy was soon settled in Nebraska. Anyone who wanted to go without a tie was welcome to do so, but it was not a matter of doctrine. (Strange how things go full circle. Now we have young pastors who wear attractive sport shirts with sweaters when they preach on Sunday morning, and those of us who have been in the ministry for years know this is heresy but have not been able to find the scriptural or historical references good enough to prove our point.)

There was a time in my church fellowship when working on Sunday, bowling, "mixed swimming," billiards and playing cards were prohibited by the fellowship (or at least "frowned upon"). They, like the necktie controversy, have had their time and judged not to be essential matters for decisions by the church, best left to individual choice.

Not all conscience questions are as easily resolved. It is difficult in some instances to decide whether a particular behavior is a conscience question or a nonnegotiable doctrine. A few of the subjects we shall mention are considered by many Christians to be nonnegotiable stands of the church, irreducible and scripturally based. Many other Christians consider them conscience questions and the decision about them best left to individuals and families.

Prayer in schools has become a subject on which edicts are made from the pulpit and by church committees. On the other hand, it is a conscience question for many thoughtful Christians who observe that prayer in homes and in churches is still not practiced by many, our country is religiously diverse, and students can individually observe moments of silent prayer any time they wish. At one time attending movies was a sin in the church fellowship of my youth, but television forced us to acknowledge what was always true: watching movies is a matter of conscience, though information and suggestions about movies are welcomed by most Christians.

Abortion is a horrible practice and unacceptable as a method of birth control and, thereby, population control. Yet many Christians are not ready to identify with those who have reduced this major social issue to simplistic answers. Thoughtful Christians are not ready to get on pro-life or pro-choice bandwagons when the rhetoric is inflammatory and respect and reason are abandoned. Abortion has implications for every part of our life, including moral and spiritual implications. Ways to approach the problem of abortion must allow some room for the expression and exercise of an individual's freedom as a citizen and for a Christian conscience. No one whom I have heard has all the answers on this issue.

Mrs. Foglesong convinced me when I was a teenager to sign a temperance pledge indicating that I would never drink alcoholic beverages. The church of which I am a part considers abstinence a Christian discipline. I am thankful that I have had the encouragement not to drink alcohol and the support system for my commitment. I can think of two occasions that I drank an ounce of wine for "the stomach's sake" (1 Timothy 5:23). My church and I are greatly concerned about alcohol abuse. Yet, perhaps we would be wiser to allow more liberty of conscience than we have. Members of our fellowship who live in Europe drink wine and beer. Many fellow Christians in the USA drink wine. "Alcohol abuse is rightfully a concern of the church, but a new consideration of what is a matter of conscience and what is not would be appropriate" was the comment recently by a pastor of conservative persuasions in North Carolina.

Often the line is not easily drawn between matters of essential belief and matters of conscience. One of the subjects on which a variety of opinions exists is homosexuality and gay lifestyle. A few of my closest friends say such behavior is a matter of conscience based on human factors beyond the control of the gay person. It is my belief that gay persons must not be denied any provision or service of our government or society and that the church must be aggressively open in ministering to gay persons.

I stop at that point, and my friends believe me to be in error. It is my conviction that the Bible and the church have consistently identified homosexual and lesbian lifestyles as unacceptable; therefore, persons practicing the gay lifestyle are not eligible for leadership in a congregation.

This is a difficult one for me, for I love and appreciate my friends who are gay, but I feel the church has the responsibility and privilege of stating those practices that limit a person's participation in leadership, even if it includes matters such as attendance to movies, consumption of alcoholic beverages, or sexual practices. The church may come to confess error, but it should not abandon prohibitions that it believes essential to the maintenance of the faith. As stated, where the line is drawn is a difficult and sobering responsibility for congregational leaders. It is not difficult to state unequivocally that all persons are to be treated in the church with love and respect—everyone!

Richard Willowby says it better than I. He encourages a compassionate and open ministry to all persons, including homosexuals, but concludes:

> The church, in biblical, theological, scientific, and sociological dialogue needs to set the boundaries of acceptable behavior for homosexuals who follow Christ, just as over centuries it has set the boundaries of acceptable behavior for heterosexuals.
> (*Vital Christianity*, November 1997, 27)

Even so, I am committed to continuing study and conversations with my Christian friends who believe sexual orientation is, if not specifically, more in the nature of a conscience question.

Each group of Christians has the right to determine what are matters of essential doctrine and what are matters of conscience. Some decisions may appear to be ridiculous to peers and subsequent generations. It is worth noting, however, Holiness groups for years have insisted that the use of tobacco is harmful to the physical body and not a habit consistent with the Christian lifestyle but now that cause is more emphatically and militantly stated by the medical profession. That which appeared odd and sectish has proven to be wise. On the other hand, medical science has made us aware that fat diets and obesity are harmful to the physical body and Holiness churches have not always accepted that equally important insight for the human body.

The concern here is that people are priority and maintaining relationships and ministry to people is more important than agreement on every issue. Teaching and leadership positions are related to foundational theological issues and each group must be clear in defining who may serve in these positions. Even persons who, to my mind, are in doctrinal error still deserve to be known, appreciated, served, related to, heard, loved, and honored.

Freedom to Be a Pilgrim

This may be at the heart of all the freedoms we have been talking about. At no one time is everyone in a congregation at the same place in his or her personal and spiritual pilgrimage. Mature Christians who have served the Lord for years as disciplined disciples may have a set of concerns that the new Christian has never considered and probably is not ready to consider.

Each of us is on a spiritual journey and as we enjoy fellowship in the church we participate in a covenant to assist each other on the journey. I have eight grandchildren and each is growing in skills and interests but not at the same pace and not with skills in the same areas. Leah, for instance has always had mature ways. Kinsey, like her cousin Leah, has been an athlete. Kinsey's sister Whitney is riding horses and her four-year-old brother Cole smiles as he tells you, "I can can pitch a baseball really fast." Four-year-old Brianna is not yet quite as perceptive about the world as her seven year-old-brother Dustin, but she is developing very winsome characteristics that will endear her to many. Similar observations can be made about Brady, who seems never to meet a stranger and plays soccer well, and Annie who has obvious gifts for taking charge of any situation. They are not at the same stages of development in academics, athletics, personality, and relationships, and we would not want them to be. It is a shame when we expect children and young people to learn certain things by certain ages and master certain disciplines at a certain age because someone else did.

In the life of the church each Christian is at a different stage of development. One who is a relatively new Christian may give evidence of discipleship that is only now being experienced by another who has been a

Christian for seven years. That is okay! It is desirable that each person grow at a pace that allows for a mature Christianity rather than a neurotic spirituality.

FREEDOM AND ACCOUNTABILITY

Freedom and accountability are a part of each other. Discipleship is our response to grace; it is in the context of accountability that we genuinely experience freedom. "Accountability" is a chapter in the book *Hi-Q Christians*. Five guides for accountability are identified:

• The *Bible* is one guide for accountability (2 Timothy 3:16).

• The *conscience* is a guide for accountability (Jeremiah 31:31–34).

• Membership in the body of Christ, the *church*, is a structure for accountability (Acts 2:37–47).

• Participation in a *small group* of Christians is another.

• The *pastor* is a special person in the Christian's accountability structure.

My church and my pastor are responsible to hold me accountable for (1) worship, (2) my lifestyle, (3) my ministry, and (4) my relationships. The follower of Jesus Christ chooses to be accountable.

—Summarized from *Hi-Q Christians* (58–73)

A mature faith is desirable, and we are encouraged to grow; however, particular joys are a part of each stage of discipleship. The enthusiasm and excitement that are often a part of being a new Christian are not always present as one matures. The idealism that captivates the imagination and vision of a Christian deciding on a vocation will be tempered by the real-life experience of service in that vocation.

Freedom to be a pilgrim is a marvelous gift the church can give each of us—permitting us to explore, venture, learn, and rejoice. It is great to be on a journey; it is disheartening to be poured into a mold.

The instructions of the Book of Hebrews are for us all:

> Therefore let us go on toward perfection, leaving behind the basic teaching about Christ, and not laying again the foundation: repentance from dead works and faith toward God, instruction about baptisms, laying on of hands, resurrection of the dead, and eternal judgment.
> (Hebrews 6:1)

Paul put it in different words for the Christians at Ephesus:

> We must no longer be children, tossed to and fro and blown about by every wind of doctrine, by people's trickery, by their craftiness in deceitful scheming. But speaking the truth in love, we must grow up in every way into him who is the head, into Christ, from whom the whole body, joined and knit together by every ligament with which it is equipped, as each part is working properly, promotes the body's growth in building itself up.
> (Ephesians 4:14–16)

Ponder and Process

Action Process
Listen intently to five persons this week (see definition of empathic listening in chapter 2: "People are Priority"). Write below the names of the persons to whom you have intently listened.

Meditation Process
Think through a conscience question that is a difficult one for you.

Discussion Process
Ask the group to read silently the following scriptures: James 2:2–4; Hebrews 6:1; Ephesians 4:14–16. Keep in mind, persons search for scriptures at different speeds; others may need suggestions on how to find the reference. Encourage comments and questions on the scriptures.

Enlist three persons in the group to tell where they are in their spiritual pilgrimages. Have others indicate with which of the three persons they presently identify in their own spiritual quest.

Encourage participants to get in groups of three, each identify where he or she is in a Christian pilgrimage, and then each pray for the one to the right.

Chapter 11

SINNERS, SLIDERS, SAINTS, AND THE SLIGHTED

The church that puts people first will provide special ministries to at least five categories of people. Before the categories are identified, however, I will state my objection to placing people in categories even though I have done so in previous chapters.

I am a religious person, but that identification does not fully encompass my life and interests. I also have secular interests such as sports, reading, photography, and movies that I could do without and not affect my religious nature. On the other hand, many persons have interest in all four of these secular fields who would not necessarily be a part of a religious organization. I am a religious person but I also have secular interests.

The sacred/secular categorization becomes even more exacting when people discover I am a Christian clergyperson. Persons apologize for using "four letter words" when they learn I am a pastor. A person with a graduate education and wide experience expressed surprise when I told him that I not only paid taxes but gave offerings to the church; he was convinced that pastors neither tithed nor were taxed. A few others seem unaware that Christian ministers have sexual interests, evidently convinced that all four of my children were immaculate conceptions. More than a few believe that pastors should never be angry or lack faith. None of those expectations or characterizations are serious but they dehumanize; they place me in a category that could restrict my enjoyment of life.

I don't like being placed in a category for it does not take seriously my uniqueness, and I expect most persons feel the same way. We say, "I am not a number; I am somebody, not something!"

Recognizing that none of us like being thought of as just one of a group of persons, still it is helpful to identify some general groups of people with whom the church has great interest and whose individual needs can be met if the groups are identified. The sensitive church will serve five rather broadly defined groups present in most fellowships: sinners, backsliders, two groups of saints, and the slighted.

We now will look at the groups of persons in the local church who need specific and special attention: Sinners, Sliders, Saints, and the Slighted.

Sinners, Group #1

It is true that in one way of thinking we are all sinners "since all have sinned and fall short of the glory of God" (Romans 3:23). Sinners, Group #1, refers to those persons who have not accepted Jesus Christ as Savior and Lord. They may have a belief in God and Jesus in a general way but they have not accepted forgiveness

Builders, Boomers, and Busters

These three words are categories of people with which the church is concerned: sociological categories by generation.

The Boomer generation, the largest ever, numbers more than 76 million in the United States, one third of our nation's population. The Boomers are persons born between 1946 and 1964. They have a group identity distinct from that of the previous generation, including a hesitancy to associate with traditional churches.

Builders is one of the names given to the generation that experienced the two World Wars, lived through the Depression, and knew that hard work could accomplish about anything. They are the parents and grandparents of the Boomers and many are committed to church organizations.

Still another generation is the Busters, born between 1965 and 1984, and so named because there were fewer of them than the Boomers even though they are the second largest generation ever, numbering about 65 million. The Busters (and they have many other names) have known television all their lives, grown up using computers, and generally are disillusioned with some of the ideals and programs of the Boomers as well as with those of Builders. Their interests are often discernible in the ways they prefer to worship and the music they enjoy.

It is important that we recognize these three general groups of people, their different mind-sets and different lifestyles. Each generation, though, has a number of distinguished and faithful Christians and all need the love and grace that is in Jesus Christ.

Several students of the three generations have written about the church's responsibility to recognize the needs of each of these groups and to develop ministries that will reach each of the generations. One of the best resources for a church to use to study the generation phenomenon is a book by Gary L. McIntosh, *Three Generations*. We acknowledge these important sociological groupings are of great importance to the church.

through Christ and have not committed to serve God. This is the second most neglected group in the life of the church. The most neglected group will be identified later.

Sinners, persons who have not accepted Christ as Savior, need information about the gospel. The good news is that God loves every person and wants to relate to everyone. Each person needs to know that in Christ we can be forgiven. Each person needs to know that Christ calls him or her to be a part of the fellowship of worshipers and believers. The task is called evangelism but, by whatever name, the sinner has a need to know that sin is a desperate situation and to hear about the salvation in Jesus Christ.

Each person has a divine right and deserves to hear the gospel in a way he or she can understand: a child, at whatever age it interests the child; a youth, at an age when spiritual interests are high; a young adult, when purpose for life is being considered; and the elderly, when the meaning of life is being discovered in a new dimension; all deserve to hear.

The sinner has a right to know that salvation is more than a ticket to eternity; it is a gateway to a new life: "If anyone is in Christ, there is a new creation: everything old has passed away; see, everything has become new" (2 Corinthians 5:17).

Ron Sider repeats the story of Michael and Addie Banks. Reverend Banks, pastor of a black congregation, was speaking to a group of denominational leaders when he related that twenty years ago, before he was a Christian, his own marriage was about dead. His job as a counselor produced exceptional stress and he drank a lot. He and Addie often spoke harshly and hurt each other.

Addie accepted Christ one day and, though she continued to be angry, she responded to Michael in a different way than she had before. Michael was surprised and he soon accepted Christ. The conversions did not resolve their marriage problems. They continued to quarrel, so one day he said, "Why don't you go your way and I'll go mine!"

> **Ways to Reach the Unchurched**
> The first, and most successful, is for churched people to build honest, caring relationships with nonchurched people and eventually to invite them to attend the church. The second is for the church to sponsor nonreligious events such as sports leagues, community fairs, social extravaganzas, community assistance projects, and concerts or seminars of interest to the nonchurched, and to invite those who attend the activities to consider attending the church's services.
> A third possibility is sending top-quality brochures about the church to people's homes to inform them and to invite them to attend the church.
> —George Barna (1995, 64)

Addie answered just as strongly, "If God has reconciled us to himself but cannot reconcile us to each other, then the whole thing is a fraud." The Good News invites sinners to enter a new kingdom in which the "Holy Spirit works both within persons and between persons. Salvation then includes the transformed marriage of new Christians like Michael and Addie Banks" (Sider 81–82).

Pollster George Barna says that the church is failing to communicate the gospel to non-Christians because they (1) "do not see the relevance of the gospel," (2) "do not comprehend what we are trying to say," and (3) the solution provided by Jesus Christ is "so different from ... solutions they are searching for."

Barna says we should not conclude that these unchurched people have heard and understood the gospel. He says, "we do ... have a responsibility to present the gospel in a fashion that can be understood, clearly and easily." His estimate is that the number of unchurched people in America is 187 million; others have estimates ranging as low as 90 million, but even that figure indicates the United States is one of the greatest missions opportunities in the world (Barna, *Evangelism,* 22, 40, 43, 44).

Dieter Zander speaks of his efforts to create a ministry to Busters, or Generation X, at the church with the largest attendance in the United States, Willow Creek Community Church in South Barrington, Illinois. He and Gary McIntosh, another well informed person on this subject, agree that the church has a great opportunity with Busters. He says, "For Busters, family is more frequently defined as those who will love them, not those who produced them."

Zander explains,

> To reach busters means someone will need to spend time with them, someone who feels comfortable sharing why he or she became a Christian, someone willing to expose the work of Christ in his or her life. This approach is labor intensive.
>
> (40–41)

Living a new life in a new kingdom is the opportunity that most people are looking for. The church has the story and the Savior, and can give the invitation.

Sinners, Group #2: Sliders

Backsliders is a term used to describe persons who have once been committed followers of Christ and part of the church but who have broken that relationship. Persons may indicate they are no longer living a dedicated Christian life, or their lifestyle may indicate to the congregation that they are not in harmony with the teachings and expectations of the local fellowship. Demas, a character in the New Testament, is an example of a backslider. Paul says of him, "For Demas, in love with this present world, has deserted me" (2 Timothy 4:10).

We acknowledge that one group of Christians (of the Calvinist theological tradition) believe that if one has accepted Christ, regardless of what happens that person does not fall from saving grace. Christians of another persuasion (those who align more nearly with the teachings of Arminius) believe that a person who returns to a sinful way of life is a backslider, fallen from grace. I am a part of the second group and believe it is possible to backslide. At the same time, I think many of us on my side of the theological fence have been too ready to think a person has fallen from grace and is no longer a Christian for insufficient reasons—such as during periods of doubt, which are a very human experience.

Whatever the theological persuasion, in the local church persons who have neglected the practice of their faith or who are living a sinful lifestyle need the ministry of the church. In each congregation a number of persons are in this group.

The church can encourage backsliders to deal with their sins and renew their commitment to Christ. The local church does this well when it has simply stated guidelines for participation in the fellowship (membership) and when it teaches the biblical standards for moral living.

The church meets the needs of backsliders when it provides ways for concerned persons, including pastors, to initiate conversations with backsliders about their spiritual situation. The initiative must be taken with compassionate understanding of the person and focus on the ways he or she can be reenlisted as a committed disciple. The pastor of a strong congregation in Indianapolis explained to me, "We are here to redeem and restore." That is the theme of congregations who minister well to those who have strayed from their faith.

Saints, Group #1: The Exemplary

A wag once said that a saint is someone who is both good and dead.

Canonization by the Catholic church takes place over a long period of time, and persons are long departed before they are recognized as saints. The designation "saints," however, was used by the Apostle Paul in reference to believers who were "called to be saints" (Romans 1:7 and 1 Corinthians 1:2) and those who in fact were living a godly life whatever their residence, "including all the saints throughout Achaia" (2 Corinthians 1:1; also Ephesians, Philippians, and Colossians). It is biblical and appropriate to use saints as an identification for the faithful followers of Christ, though it more often is used in reference to a group than to an individual, saints rather than saint.

Congregations often have a few persons whose commitment to Christ and his church is dynamic and dramatic. They are exemplary Christians whose witness is known and accepted not only in the church fellowship but in the broader community—on the job or in the school. The exemplary follower of Christ is familiar with the scripture, prays regularly and often with fervency, repeatedly accepts leadership roles in the life of the church, and lives a life that is generally acknowledged as genuinely Christian. I have been the pastor of such persons and could well use one of them as an example but will tell you instead of a couple who have been colleagues for years.

Maurice and Dondeena are exemplary saints. They will be embarrassed to read this, as much for what it could imply about their age, as anything else. They served for years as missionaries in Mexico and Brazil and were instrumental in starting schools for young adults, especially to train pastors. Maurice was personally involved in the United States civil rights movement when many of us were trying to understand what was happening. He is also an ardent pacifist, but thoughtful in discussions with persons who see things differently.

Dondeena has served as a missionary, has a bright and positive expression of faith in Christ, and has been deeply committed to the church. Though undoubtedly at times questioning the church's priorities, she has served it with a commitment to excellence. Together they have led hundreds of college students and adults in missions work camps in several countries. Maurice and Dondeena have not escaped injury, heartache, and disappointment, however. In our church fellowship, when one thinks of Latin American missions and positive voices, one thinks of Maurice and Dondeena. They are exemplary saints.

The exemplary saints have needs that can be met only by an alert and insightful congregation. Exemplary saints are human and need encouragement, time for themselves, assignments consistent with their gifts, prayers for strength, and an understanding listener on occasion, just like anyone else. Exemplary saints are a treasure but they are human and their needs must be met; they, too, must be supported with prayer and words of encouragement.

Saints, Group #2: Good People

Many persons are faithful followers of Christ, real saints in a less obvious way. They are people who have committed themselves to the Lord and his church but whose Christian example and humble spirit are known less broadly. Their friends, neighbors, fellow workers, and associates know their Christian influence but their witness and names are not known far beyond the church membership or neighborhood. They, too, would be embarrassed to be called saints but they are persons who for years have lived a good life, spoken kind words, prayed for persons in need, given of their financial resources, and sustained congregations by their faithfulness in prosperous and difficult times.

Paul Dortmund comes to my mind, among several I could mention. He managed a hardware store and seemed always to be doing favors for a customer or listening to the woes of a friend. He was not often up front in church meetings but most of the things of great importance that happened in the church the ten years I was his pastor, he helped initiate or saw to it that they were done well. Paul worked wonders with wood. Two candleholders in my bedroom were made by Paul from the decking of the first unit of the Meadow Park Church in Columbus, Ohio—a building about which both he and I often dreamed together. Paul wanted everything in the church done like those beautiful candleholders, "nice and right." He had a way of encouraging persons with comments that were generous but not embarrassing. He inquired about the welfare of individuals, often asking me about Laura or one of our children, by name. He was not afraid of risk but sought to avoid confrontation in diplomatic ways.

Paul was a good man whose goodness at the hardware store, in the community, and in the church gave security to many of us. We relied on him for a listening ear and advice. The famous Christian author Elton Trueblood surprised me once in a very brief conversation by telling me of his appreciation for Paul's friendship. Paul had a keen sense of humor and were he to comment on what I have written, would observe, "Pastor, I noticed you said that a saint is someone who is *good and dead*."

The good people keep a church going. They were

Sinners, Sliders, Saints, and the Slighted

Christians when we first knew them and they are Christians today. They made sacrifices for the kingdom before and they will make them again. They will know and encourage leaders who emerge, though rarely accepting positions of prominence for themselves. They are the encouragers, the supporters, the faithful, the kind, the thoughtful persons in the local church who are committed to Christ. No one ever questions that fact.

They are so faithful that a local church may overlook the attention they need. One reason they may be overlooked: they are so faithful and kind that we presume they have no special needs. But they do!

The faithful saints need the encouragement of sermons and lessons that are reflected in the words of a hymn:

> Does the place you're called to labor
>   Seem so small and little known?
> It is great if God is in it,
>   And He'll not forget His own.
> Little is much when God is in it,
>   Labor not for wealth or fame;
> There's a crown and you can win it,
>   If you go in Jesus' name.
> (*Worship the Lord*: *Hymnal of the Church of God*, 565)

The exemplary, adventuresome, up-front saints, though they are few, often get accolades from the church. The exemplary saints may receive notices in the newspaper, be honored for years of service with banquets, and lifted up as examples for young people. The saints who are just good, faithful members of the congregation rarely are honored—so, it is important that the pastor and other leaders regularly point out the significant role of those who are the faithful saints, the good people.

Another special ministry this second group of saints needs is challenge. These are the persons who may spend years in the same assignment. They may be a Sunday school teacher for twenty years, an usher for eighteen, or a nursery worker for eleven years. The faithful good saints may be unaware that they have other abilities. A change may be both refreshing to them and rewarding for the congregation. Harry and Marilyn Smothers were excellent volunteer youth ministers in a church I pastored. After several years in that responsibility they suggested the church call a youth minister and they began to address themselves to broader participation in the life of the church. For Harry this included membership on a national publication board of the church. As their pastor, I resisted the idea of the change but their lives were enriched and other areas of ministry were enhanced because of the change.

The group of Saints #2 needs all the ministries that other members need. It is the easiest group to take for granted. A church is greatly strengthened when these good people are made aware of the importance of their ministries and, occasionally, challenged to consider other areas of service.

The Slighted People

The slighted people are the most consistently neglected persons. Sinners are the second most neglected but churches usually acknowledge that sinners should be evangelized. Backsliders will, in due time, get some attention even if the attention is tardy and poorly given. Saints are a part of the congregation and their interests will surface and be met in several ways. The slighted are often totally forgotten. Local churches may not even be aware that slighted persons are a part of their ministry; the church may be more aware of slighted persons who live in a foreign country than the ones who live in their neighborhood.

> **The Chicago Declaration of Evangelicals**
> We acknowledge that God requires justice. But we have not proclaimed or demonstrated his justice to an unjust American society. Although the Lord calls us to defend the social and economic rights of the poor and oppressed, we have mostly remained silent. We deplore the historic involvement of the church in America with racism and the conspicuous responsibility of the evangelical community for perpetuating the personal attitudes and institutional structures that have divided the body of Christ along color lines.
> We call our fellow evangelical Christians to demonstrate repentance in a Christian discipleship that confronts the social and political injustice of our nation.
> —Quoted in Ronald Sider (19)

Slighted persons are people who get less attention when they are born. They have inadequate food as a baby and child, they receive less medical attention and get medicine only in extreme emergencies. They live in poorly furnished homes and have minimal clothing. They have less food and few, if any, gifts on holidays like Christmas or birthdays. They may receive little discipline and a lot of punishment, not only at home but at school and in society. They rarely enjoy a vacation trip. They have no political power, except as they are used for a politician's purposes. They have little access to legal services. Little special training is provided for them. If slighted people fail in school or commit a crime, it was "expected" by society and they usually get the harshest sentences. In every way the slighted get less than everyone else.

Here's the clincher! They are slighted by the church, also. It is true that many of the most significant ministries to the desperately needy people in the United States are provided through churches: transient homes, hot meals, clothing distribution, and, in a few situations, schooling. We must acknowledge that even churches who do well in emergency type ministries often fail to encourage members to vote and influence legislation in ways that make the suffering of the slighted more endurable and their opportunities more fair.

Patty was a slighted one I knew in elementary school. She lived two blocks further than I did from Little Page School where we were in the same class, so she passed by our house on the way to school. In the winter she wore a thin dress and coat that was an obvious hand-me-down. She didn't have leggings to wear like the rest of us. Her family lived in a small rented house that looked cold and bare. Her hair was cut in bangs, not bangs that were attractive but that made her look shaggy and unkempt. Her school books were never new ones and showed signs of wear. She was shy to the point of almost total silence. Her grades were poor and she received fewer cards than the rest of us on Valentine's Day. We did not live high-on-the-hog ourselves, but she was poor. Not a year goes by that I don't recall Patty and how much my heart ached for her. She was slighted. We moved from that neighborhood when I was twelve years old and I did not see Patty again. I have hoped that Patty had opportunities for happiness as a teenager and adult, but I know the odds are she didn't. Slighted people usually continue to be slighted.

It is of such persons that Jesus speaks to the church today as he spoke to his followers during his earthly ministry, when he challenged them to welcome strangers, feed the hungry, clothe the needy, and serve those who were sick and in prison: "Just as you did not do it to one of the least of these, you did not do it to me" (Matthew 25:45).

Too often in the '90s churches must honestly confess, "We failed!"

Pastor John Harvey, mentioned in a previous chapter, has a concern for people whom our financial/economic system tends to bypass. A letter from John provides insight into the genius of his ministry to the slighted:

> A total of sixteen homes have been rehabilitated in the Chelsea neighborhood in Kansas City, Kansas. Fourteen of these homes have been sold to low/moderate income first-time homeowners. (The other two homes are being leased.) Each of these new homeowners graduated from our Homebuyer Education Program and is receiving follow-up assistance and training.

Sixteen other homeowners received home improvement grants, and the rehabilitation and construction of new homes is scheduled for the Turtle Hill neighborhood. Nathaniel and Dana and their daughters had dreamed of owning a home and saved toward that goal, but their loan applications were repeatedly rejected. City Vision Ministries, created by Pastor Harvey, made a way for them to purchase a four-bedroom home for their growing family. The slighted were enabled.

Richard Prim also pastors in the Kansas City area. The recent addition of a new facility was named to honor a sixteen-year-old boy who was slain as he entered the church one Sunday morning. The event challenged the congregation to a greater involvement in a ministry focused on black males in the inner city. A young man came forward in one worship service and gave Pastor Prim a gun, indicating he wanted to give up violence and live for Christ. The scene was repeated with another young man a few weeks later. The slighted are being served.

Another example, this one from Cincinnati: Dayspring Church asked itself a few years ago "How do we speak to and minister to our community?" The members of the church contacted persons living in the community and asked them about their perceptions of the church. They learned that the church was regarded as a big church that needed nothing, even more so, "A big white [Caucasian] church on the corner whose 'fence and gate' keep us out!" The church decided they did not want to be a "white church" but the body of Christ serving the community.

They opened their beautiful family life center on Monday nights to the community. King's Court began as a basketball ministry and ninety percent of the participants were African American's. Starting with about ten youth, the ministry now includes more than 150. Tutoring in public school subjects was added to the ministry as well as arts, crafts, and Bible lessons for the younger children. Then came drill teams, jump rope teams, musical groups, and a food program. A devotional time each evening includes an opportunity to accept Christ. Pastor Mitchell Burch says, "Our church has grown with greater participation of ethnic groups in the neighborhood and cross-cultural experiences. Now many members of our church are from the community."

The slighted, denied access to a wonderful facility in their own community, became the blessed, as the church opened its facilities for recreation and worship and provided ministries to youth and children.

Conclusion

The train headed north out of Dacca, Bangladesh, with my five traveling companions and me. We stopped briefly after an hour or so to pick up passengers. Just as the train started to move again, a person with severe handicaps came into view. None of us could take our eyes from him. He had no arms and no legs, yet he was "walking" while lying on his back, twisting his shoulder blades and hips so that they became the four feet that mobilized him. He moved with amazing quickness and purposefulness.

My pity went out to the man but then I began to marvel at how his intellect, his will, and his physical discipline enabled him to survive in a nation where even those who are physically whole have a hard time obtaining necessities. My mind went further: in the world that I knew the man could have at least a chair, even a motorized one, and perhaps artificial arms and legs, prostheses, that would enable him to move about with a semblance of normality. The chairs, the prosthesis, the know-how, the therapy are available in our world, but the man whom I saw for only a few seconds that day probably doesn't know about them. Even if he did, he would not know how to obtain them.

People in our churches, our neighborhoods, in our cities, and in our towns are also handicapped but in a far more devastating way. They do not know of the salvation that is in Christ and the meaning that comes to life when one worships and lives for God. Persons whom you and I know have habits that destroy their minds. They have attitudes that wreck their relationships. They live deprived lives for they do not know that God loves them; many are convinced that God does not love them.

The church has the resource that can make all the difference. The information the church has will enable them to walk in ways they cannot walk now. The provision of which the church is aware can enable a sense of purpose and meaning they have never known. It begins with the simple message, "For God so loved the world that he gave his only Son, so that everyone who believes in him may not perish but may have eternal life" (John 3:16). They and we repeatedly misunderstand. We think that God loves us if we behave ourselves. Certainly God calls us to live a quality life but the secret is this: "God proves his love for us in that while we still were sinners Christ died for us" (Romans 5:8).

People need to hear that information from the church. Each person in the church is refreshed and encouraged by the knowledge that God loves us, not because of something we have done but God just loves us. Millions of people will be enabled to walk in ways they never dreamed of if we will put people first in the life and ministry of the church and let them know for sure that God loves them.

More than ever before in my life, I am discovering hundreds of congregations that are determined to place people first and put buildings, traditions, egos, and social status in proper perspective—biblical perspective. I am encouraged and thrilled about what is happening in so many congregations that honor the name of the Lord and serve the people the Lord loves.

Ponder and Process

Action Process
Encourage a group in which you participate to make a list of the "slighted" persons in your community and identify ways your church may serve them.

Meditation Process
Pray, "Lord, I want to be more open to the needs of all people. What changes in my attitude will be necessary?"

Discussion Process
Enlist one person to read Matthew 25:37–40 and a second to read Galatians 6:1–10. Encourage comments and questions.

List the names for the three generations on a chalkboard or newsprint indicating in parenthesies the birth years: **Builders** (before 1946), **Boomers** (1946–1964), and **Busters** (1965–1983). Identify two or three persons in your church for each age group and then list some of the ways they differ in lifestyle, use of money, entertainment, and preference in mode of worship. How can the church be appreciative of the interests of all generations and minister to each at the level of felt needs?

Identify the slighted in your community. What opportunity does your congregation have for ministry with the slighted?

Using a large sheet of paper, perhaps newsprint, write a prayer together. Thank the Lord for answered prayers in your group. Include the concerns you have for your local church and for individuals who are close relatives or friends of persons in your group. You may want to conclude the prayer as follows:

> Now may the Lord of peace himself give you peace at all times in all ways. The Lord be with you all (2 Thessalonians 3:16). Amen.

Form a circle, hold hands, and read the prayer.

BIBLIOGRAPHY

Albrecht, Karl. *Stress and the Manager: Making It Work for You*. New York: A Touchstone Book, Published by Simon and Schuster, Inc., 1979.

Alexander, John. "The Other Side," *Christianity Today*, January 9, 1995, 36.

Augsburger, Myron S. *The Communicator's Commentary: Matthew*. Lloyd J. Ogilvie, general editor. Waco, Tex: Word Books, 1982.

Barclay, William. "The Gospel of Matthew," vol. 2. *The Daily Study Bible Series*. Philadelphia: Westminster Press, 1958.

Barna, George. *Evangelism That Works*. Ventura, Calif: Regal Books, a Division of GL Publications, 1995.

———*Today's Pastors*. Ventura, Calif: Regal Books, a Division of GL Publications, 1993.

Bruner, Frederick Dale. *The Christbook, A Historical Theological Commentary*, Matthew 1—12. Waco, Tex: Word Books, 1987.

Buttrick, George Arthur, general editor. *Interpreter's Dictionary of the Bible*, vol. 2. New York: Abingdon Press, 1962.

Carson, D. A. "Matthew." *Expositor's Bible Commentary*. vol. 8. Frank E. Goebelin, general editor. Grand Rapids: Zondervan, Regency Reference Library, 1984.

Carter, Stephen L. *The Culture of Disbelief*. New York: Basic Books, a Division of Harper Collins, 1993.

Covey, Stephen R. *The 7 Habits of Highly Effective People.* New York: Simon and Schuster, 1989.

Congregations: The Alban Journal. Washington, DC: Alban Institute

Craig, Grace J. *Human Development,* 4th ed. Englewood Cliffs, New Jersey: Prentice-Hall, 1986.

Crowell, Rodney J. *Musical Pulpits.* Grand Rapids: Baker Book House, 1992.

Dunham, Maxie. *The Workbook of Intercessory Prayer.* Nashville: Upper Room Publishers, 1979.

Foster, Richard J. *Prayer: Finding the Heart's True Home.* San Francisco: Harper, 1992.

Friedman, Edwin H. *Generation to Generation.* New York: The Guilford Press, 1985.

Gallup, George, Jr. *National and International Religion Report* vol. 5, no. 11 (May 20, 1991): 1.

Groff, Kent Ira. *Congregations,* (Nov—Dec 1993): 7.

Guinness, Os and John Seel, editors. *No God But God: Breaking with the Idols of Our Age.* Chicago: Moody Press, 1992.

Hart, Archibald D. *Adrenaline and Stress.* Waco, Tex: Word Book Publisher, 1986.

Hines, Samuel G. quoted in "Reconciliation Initiative," *Vital Christianity,* April 1995, 29.

Hybels, Bill. "Standing in the Crossfire." *Leadership* vol. 16, no. 1 (winter 1993): 19–15.

Kirkpatrick, Thomas G. *Small Groups in the Church.* Washington, DC: an Alban Institute Publication, 1995.

Littauer, Florence. *Personality Plus.* Revised. Grand Rapids: Fleming H. Revell, a Division of Baker Book House, 1992.

Bibliography

Lyon, James. *Northweek.* Anderson, Ind: North Anderson Church of God.

Marty, Martin. *Context.* Chicago: Claretian Press, n.d.

Maslow, A. H. *Motivation and Personality,* 2nd ed. New York: Harper and Row, summarized in Grace J. Craig, 1984, *Human Development,* 4th ed. Englewood Cliffs, NJ: Prentice Hall, 1954.

Mead, Loren. "Learning Points: An Interview with Loren Mead." *Christian Century* (March 23–30, 1994): 310–312.

McIntosh, Gary L. *Three Generations.* Grand Rapids: Fleming H. Revell, a Division of Baker Book House Co, 1995.

Moore, Thomas. *Care of the Soul.* NY: Harper Perennial, a Division of Harper Collins Publishers, 1992.

Morgan, Marlo. *Mutant Message Down Under.* New York: Harper Collins Publishers, 1994.

Oates, Wayne C. *The Care of Troublesome People.* Washington, DC: an Alban Institute Publication, 1994.

Olsen, Charles M. *Transforming Church Boards.* Washington, DC: an Alban Institute Publication, 1995.

Oppenheimer, J. Robert. quoted in *Time,* April 25, 1994, 65.

Oswald, Roy M. and Otto Kroeger. *Personality Types and Religious Leadership.* Washington, DC: an Alban Institute Publication, 1990.

Peck, M. Scott. *The Different Drum: Community-Making and Peace.* New York: Simon and Schuster, 1987.

Sider, Ronald J. *One-Sided Christianity?* Grand Rapids: Zondervan Publishing and San Francisco: Harper, San Francisco, Divisions of Harper Collins Publishers, 1993.

Stevens, R. Paul and Phil Collins. *The Equipping Pastor.* Washington, DC: an Alban Institute Publication, 1993.

Swindoll, Charles R. *The Grace Awakening.* Dallas: Word Publishing, 1993.

The Interpreter's Dictionary of the Bible, s.v. "grace."

Tillapaugh, Frank R. *The Church Unleashed.* Ventura, Calif: Regal Books, a Division of GL Publications, 1982.

————*Unleashing Your Potential.* Ventura, CA: Regal Books, A Division of GL Publications, 1988.

Webster's II New Riverside Dictionary. Boston: Houghton Miflin Company, 1984.

Wilson, Edward. *Sociobiology: The New Synthesis.* Cambridge, Mass: Harvard University Press/The Belknap Press (cited by others), 1975.

Withrow, Oral. *Hi-Q Christians.* Anderson, Ind: Warner Press, 1993.

Worship the Lord: Hymnal of the Church of God. Anderson, Ind: Warner Press, 1988.

Zander, Dieter. "The Gospel for Generation X." *Leadership* vol. 16, no. 2, (spring 1995): 40–41.